A CLOUD
OF WITNESSES

Calvinistic Baptists in the 18th century

Michael Haykin

With a prologue by
David Fountain

ET Perspectives No. 3

Published by
EVANGELICAL TIMES
Faverdale North, Darlington, DL3 0PH, England

E-mail: theeditors@evangelicaltimes.org

Web: http://www.evangelicaltimes.org

First published 2006

British Library Cataloguing in Publication Data available

ISBN 0-9500129-3-9

Printed in Great Britain
by Athenaeum Press, Gateshead, UK

To Nigel & Janice Pibworth
for their Christ-like friendship
and warm fellowship
in the gospel

A CLOUD OF WITNESSES

CONTENTS page

Publisher's note   6
Author's preface   7
Prologue; the neglected years   9

1. Hercules Collins and the art of preaching   21
2. William Mitchel and itinerant evangelism   27
3. The celebrated Mrs Anne Dutton   33
4. Abraham Booth and the ethics of slavery   39
5. John Ryland Jr and the Bristol Academy   45
6. John Thomas and the mission to India   53
7. Coxe Feary and the awakening in Bluntisham   59
8. The seraphic Pearce   65
9. My dear Sarah   73
10. John Sutcliff and the prayer call of 1784   83

Publisher's Note

From time to time, *Evangelical Times*, a monthly newspaper, publishes series of articles on a variety of subjects, ranging from historical to theological, from practical Christian living to Bible exposition. The Editors feel that these series are often of sufficient interest to warrant being made available in their own right, and have therefore launched a series of booklets under the generic title ET Perspectives as a means to this end.

The main chapters of this booklet first appeared as a series of articles in *Evangelical Times* during 2001 and 2002, while the Prologue by the late Pastor David Fountain (reproduced here by kind agreement of Mrs Frances Fountain) is based on articles printed in the summer of 2001. All this material now appears in collected form as the third volume of ET Perspectives.

Our prayerful hope is that these inexpensive booklets will be of use in furthering the gospel of the glory of our Lord Jesus Christ and bringing men and women to a deeper knowledge of his unsearchable riches.

The Editors
Evangelical Times

Author's Preface

The work of God the Holy Spirit in the eighteenth century, which we call 'the Evangelical Awakening', has received a huge amount of attention over the past 250 years. This is not surprising, given its fascinating nature and profound effects. In its opening stages this revival mainly impacted the Anglicans in England and Wales and the Church of Scotland north of the border, and these sectors of Christianity have been heavily studied.

Yet — as this collection of biographical sketches seeks to show — God was also at work in other Christian communities. The Particular Baptists, for example, though not as deeply impacted by revival till later in the century, nevertheless did know the vivifying presence of God throughout this period. Reading the writings of Baptists like William Mitchel, Benjamin Beddome, Anne Dutton, and Anne Steele in the mid-eighteenth century forces one to realize that there was more spiritual fruitfulness in their circles than has been hitherto credited by historians.

This book relates the story of ongoing faithfulness among these eighteenth-century Christians, as well as the blessing that came to their communities later in that century. It is a story that never ceases to thrill, encourage and challenge me. Some of the names involved are well-known, others more obscure. All, however, speak to us across the centuries and we would do well to listen.

Of course, we do not live in their day. Our faithfulness to Christ and his gospel must have a contemporary ring to it — for this is the day in which the Lord has called us to set forth the glory of his person and work. Yet, just as knowledge of what preceded the New Testament era is vital for our understanding of the new covenant, so today we can be helped enormously to fulfil our duty and privilege as witnesses to Christ if we spend time listening to the past and seeing what God did then.

I am deeply thankful to Edgar Andrews and Andrea Whaley for preparing these articles for publication. It is also a privilege to have them introduced by the late Pastor David Fountain — from whose work on other historical figures, like Isaac Watts and Lord Radstock, I have greatly benefited. David's prologue skilfully sketches the 17th and early 18th century background to my own contributions. I am sorry I never met David in the flesh, though we did correspond and talk on the phone on various occasions. The joy of meeting him awaits eternity!

Michael Haykin
Dundas, Ontario

June 2006

Prologue

by David Fountain

THE NEGLECTED YEARS (1662-1737)

Since the first Puritan Conference was held at Westminster Chapel, Christians throughout the world have been able to explore the great inheritance left by the Puritans through reprints of their works. Special attention has also been paid to the 'Great Awakening' of the early 18th century, in which Whitefield and the Wesleys were prominent. But what about the intervening years? What do we know about the period between the 'Great Ejection' of 1662 and the 'Great Awakening' of the 1730s? We have heard of Watts, Bunyan and Doddridge. We may also know about the 1689 Baptist Confession. But what else do we know? Was nothing happening worthy of attention?

We have been told that this was a barren period. Bishop J. C. Ryle is most emphatic that this was an era when 'natural theology without a single distinctive doctrine of Christianity, cold morality or barren orthodoxy formed the staple teaching both in church and chapel. The Nonconformist body ... existed ... but could hardly be said to have lived. They did nothing, they were sound asleep'. According to Ryle, when the great change came, it 'came neither from the Church of England as a body, nor yet ... from the Dissenters. The men who wrought deliverance for us were a few individuals, most of them clergymen of the Church of England'.

The Dissenters

This negative view is shared by some Baptist historians. Others, however, offer a different picture. In his *Congregational History* Waddington writes, 'It is rather unusual for Nonconformist historians to notice the humble and almost nameless people who met in "dark conventicles". They felt a natural pride in tracing their origin to Cromwell, Owen and Baxter. None of our word-painters have attempted to sketch these village churches in the day of small things'.

Historians David Bogue and James Bennett, in their *History of the Dissenters 1688-1838*, supply what is lacking — setting an example in the way they have looked for spiritual life in their study of church history. They complain that church history has concentrated on the wrong things. 'The exterior of the church is presented to us with sufficient fullness, but the interior is not disclosed to view ... The advancement of spiritual religion in the soul, the conversion of sinners, and the edifying lives of the disciples, in the exercise of the gifts and graces of the Holy Spirit, are topics for which the reader looks almost in vain'.

Bogue and Bennett describe the Dissenters over the period 1688-1714 — 'Few in any age were better instructed in the doctrines and duties of Christianity and could give a more reasonable account of the hope that was in them. While they were content to suffer for their profession, always to be despised on account of their singularities, and frequently to endure other serious injuries, it is fair to say that the state of religion among them was prosperous'.

It cannot be denied that there was a dreadful spiritual decline among the churches during the period between the

Puritans and Methodists. Attention has been drawn to this by many historians.

But it needs to be emphasised that this was not until after the death of Queen Anne in 1714 and occurred only among particular denominations. In other areas there was growing prosperity. This neglected fact raises important questions.

The English Presbyterians

Most of the 2,000 ministers ejected from the State Church in 1662 were Presbyterians. Many of the ejected ministers were still able to preach to large congregations but their successors were men of a different character — these could imitate their predecessors in the length and weight of their discourses, but not in their power. Coldness and formality replaced evangelistic fervour and spiritual zeal. Eventually, the Presbyterian congregations shrank in size and number. By 1715 they were reduced to 600. Evangelical Presbyterianism became worldly and respectable, losing many ministers to the Church of England and large numbers from their congregations. A few sought refuge among the Independents, where they could be sure of an orthodox ministry.

In the Salters' Hall controversy of 1719, the Unitarian views of a small number of prominent Presbyterians in the West Country were exposed, but tolerance of these views by others also emerged. Men who had hitherto concealed their heresies now became bold, and false teaching came in like a flood. Within 55 years the English Presbyterian denomination was reduced to three hundred congregations.

Samuel Palmer's *London Manuscript* provides an interesting commentary on this process. When he visited London in 1731 signs of decay were clearly visible. Over half of the Presbyterian churches were no longer Calvinistic. Nearly all the young ministers had embraced Arminianism, which led to Unitarianism. Congregations were generally in decline. Eventually, English Presbyterianism virtually ceased to exist. The testimony was not finally extinguished because Scottish Presbyterians, who were very different from their English brethren, came to the assistance of the denomination in the north-east.

The Independents

However, while Presbyterianism was in decline, Independent churches were, in fact, growing throughout the country. They had reached 270 congregations in 1715 and doubled over the next fifty years. This contrast between spiritual decay among the Presbyterians and prosperity among the Independents is dealt with at some length by Bogue and Bennett, who assert, 'There was a great multitude of flourishing congregations in most parts of the country which was increasing with a steady progress. This was so remarkable in the case of Northampton and neighbouring countries that Doddridge ... says, "I know that in many of the congregations the number of Dissenters is greatly increased within these twenty years, and the interest continues ... to flourish".'

They continue, 'the religious principles of the Nonconformists were maintained by the Independents in all their purity ... There was no denomination in England which could boast of such unanimity of doctrine. Of the orthodoxy, their system of church government may be justly assigned as one powerful cause. An Independent church is, in its very nature, a society of converts ... None are admitted into that communion but such as can give satisfactory evidence that they have believed in Christ and repented of their sins, and walk as becometh the gospel'. The historians claim that from 1662 to the time of their writing in 1838, all but a few of the Independent congregations had a continued succession of gospel witness — in distinct contrast to the Anglicans and Presbyterians.

London in the early 18th century

Bogue and Bennett make an important point when they say that the Independents differed from the Presbyterians in insisting on a regenerate church membership. This comes out strongly in the *London Manuscript*. The Presbyterians were careless about who were admitted to communion. Indeed, 'some Presbyterians admitted persons into their communion by their minister's sole authority without acquainting the people with so much as their names'. By contrast, the procedure adopted by the Independents could not have been more thorough. The whole congregation had to be satisfied that all was well. With regard to discipline, 'The Presbyterians very rarely, if ever, as a church enquire into the conduct and behaviour of their members, and it is a thing almost seldom known that they discharge any of them for heresy or disorderly walking'. In doctrine, the Independents in London were Calvinists to a man. The contrast between these two denominations was very real.

The Baptists

The General Baptists were in steady decline. They were Arminian, succumbed to Unitarianism, and eventually died out, being replaced by a different Arminian group.

The Particular Baptists, on the other hand, flourished like the Independents. Bogue and Bennett tell us they 'were all Calvinists but, from want of an education for the ministry, many of them were not very judicious and some of them abused their doctrine ... On the whole, the orthodox doctrine prevailed ... and its influence appeared in the increase of many of their congregations, and in the establishing of new ones ...' *Rippon's register of Particular Baptist churches* confirms that Particular Baptist churches were flourishing throughout the country.

The Great Awakening

The generally accepted view is that the 18th Century revival came as a 'bolt from the blue' — that it was independent of what had happened previously and left 'dissent' untouched for years.

However, Kenneth Dix refers to work among the Baptists in the *early* days of the awakening. — 'I believe the work among Baptists and Independents is to be seen as a *part* of this movement and not as the *fruit* of it'. He makes the point that in 1741 in Bourton, where Benjamin Beddome was the pastor, forty people were brought to repentance at the same time. He continues: 'In ... 1753 the Particular Baptist Church at Olney covenanted together, promising, "To be maintaining in every manner of way, and in the face of all opposition whatever, the Doctrines of free grace or the faith once delivered to the Saints". But they were also concerned "for the spread and furtherance of the Gospel and increase of the knowledge of Christ in the world", and they agreed to set apart any man with gifts to the work of the ministry, "to preach the Gospel wherever God ... opens a door for him, praying for his success and wishing him God speed".

Thirty years later just such a young man was set apart for the work of the ministry. 'His name was William Carey. In other words, the fruit of the 1790s had its roots deep in the years which have been all too lightly passed by'.

Dr David L. Wykes of the Dr Williams Library states that 'during the half century preceding the Great Awakening, which is generally neglected by historians, the evangelical Church thoroughly prepared the population to anticipate, recognise and improve upon a sudden outpouring of God's grace'.

The Awakening was a genuine revival but it was preceded by a period of preparation characterised by Christ-exalting preaching. Just as the disciples entered into the labours of others (John 4:38) so the great men of church history like Wesley and Whitfield benefited from the faithful and hidden labours of others. Are we prepared to be like the unknown and unheralded men who thus prepared the ground for the Great Awakening?

Church life

Christ said he would build 'his church'. God's great purpose is to call out a people for himself. In this final section we look at the beauty of a gospel church — seeking encouraging and challenging 'role models' from this period.

We have seen that the dismal picture painted by Ryle and others is inaccurate. David L. Wykes of the Dr Williams' Library comments, 'the period between 1690 and 1715 saw tremendous growth for Dissent, so much so that I see it as the first Evangelical phase of Dissent (comparable with the Methodist Revival). During this period many new congregations were established so that by 1715 most market towns had their own meeting served by a trained minister'. But what about the quality of church life?

The Great Ejection had ended any prospect of a theocracy in England. These dissenting believers wanted a church composed of the regenerate, called out of a world that was indeed a 'wilderness' to them (Bunyan's most famous work begins, 'As I walked through the wilderness of this world'). They kept the world out by limiting membership to those who were truly saved. In consequence, the formal membership was generally only a third of those (collectively called 'hearers') who attended the church. For example, Joseph Caryl's church had 136 members in 1673, but four years earlier the census suggested that 500 attended his 'conventicle'. Congregational churches in England at this time averaged 300 hearers. The Baptists would be somewhat smaller and the Presbyterians somewhat larger, though the latter were less careful to maintain a regenerate church membership.

Great men, whose works we still enjoy, lived and

ministered in those days. The 'Prince of the Puritans', John Owen, was still guiding the people of God with his theological works.

Matthew Henry was writing his *Commentary* and Bunyan gave us *Pilgrim's Progress*. Watts' *Divine Songs* and other writings did an enormous amount of good. Those who compiled the *1689 Baptist confession* also enriched the period, making a clear biblical stand for a distinctive group of churches. In valuing this heritage let us recognise that it reflected the spiritual prosperity of the period.

Unity in the local church

Such great names inspire, but it is the churches themselves that challenge us most. Each was a united, spiritual family. Pastors were more concerned to find spiritual satisfaction among their own people than to establish reputations in the evangelical world.

Churches calling a minister from another church were deemed to be acting unlawfully if they did so without first obtaining that church's permission. The pastor was part of the family. He belonged to them. Church members were not just individuals who fancied a particular church — they were committed to one another, not just to a church programme.

Kenneth Dix describes an event In 1671. 'The Bedford Church had cause to remonstrate with a certain William Whitbread. This man had once loyally served the church in visiting its members and even administering the Word of God, but for a time ... "he had stood at a distance from them" and earnest attempts were now being made to effect his restoration'.

Dix continues, 'In one of their letters to him, they ... give an insight into what they meant by fellowship. "When did you inquire our welfare as should have become a member? When did you visit the poor, the tempted, as became a member? When did you set your shoulder to help us at any dead lift we have struck at? Have you, brother, looked diligently into the body of the church, least any root of bitterness, springing up should have defiled any? All these things are the duty of members as members, in every [one] of which you have been utterly faulty. If we should stand one from another till need was made known and help required, we should manifest but little love to, and care for, one another". This letter to brother Whitbread eventually bore fruit, for he returned to the family'.

Sincere love

In his *Glory of the gospel church*, Benjamin Keach declares that such a church 'consists in that all the saints are not only united by the Spirit of Christ but also to one another in sincere love and affection. It consists in that sweet union and concord that ought to be in the church. "By this shall all men know that ye are my disciples if you love one another" (John 13:35)'.

Dix reminds us of Bunyan's words — 'Church fellowship rightly managed is the glory of all the world. No place, no community, no fellowship is adorned and bespangled with those beauties as is the church rightly knot together to their head, and lovingly serving one another'.

Dix enlarges on what Bunyan meant by loving service — 'Believers are called and set apart to serve the Lord. They are also called to serve one another, to watch over each other, to pray for one another, to bear each other's burdens, to have a fellow feeling with each other and to recognise each other's weaknesses, failings, and infirmities. There is a need to "stir up one another to love and good works".

One means used by Dissenters to maintain the unity of the body was the Church covenant — which might include statements like, 'we ... give up ourselves to one another in the Lord, to walk together in the exercise of all those graces and discharging all those duties that are required of us as the church of Christ'. This would be read to the congregation on appropriate occasions and they would assent by adding their names or raising their hands. All this was totally consistent with Scripture. Believers are to grow up together in Christ and minister to one another (Ephesians 4:13-16).

Role models

We all need role models. The Dissenters themselves had them. Edward Winslow commented on those who would become the Mayflower Pilgrims: 'I persuade myself never people upon earth lived more lovingly together and prayed more sweetly than we the church at Leyden did'. Robinson, their pastor, said: 'If ever I saw the beauty of Zion and the glory of the Lord filling his Tabernacle, it has been in the manifestation of the diverse graces of God in the church. In that heavenly harmony and comely order wherein by the grace of God they are set and walk'.

The Independent Church at Axminster provides a wonderful role model: 'this little society continued steadfastly in a due observance of all the ordinances and institutions of the Lord Jesus Christ with gladness of heart, the Lord adding to them and increasing the number. Ah! What liveliness, what zeal forwardness in the work and ways of God, what spiritual edifying conversations, what fervent love and warm affections, what a spirit of sympathy one with another, what tender care and watchfulness over each other! What blessedness was there seen and found amongst them! What an eminent presence of God in the midst of them, what a resemblance of heaven upon earth! How amiable and lovely were their assemblies! How sweet, how profitable was a day spent in communion with them! Ah! These were espousal days. How, how delightfully could they follow God in a wilderness'.

God was truly present among his people. When the sheep are separated from the goats in Matthew 25, love for the brethren is singled out as evidence of belonging to the Lord. Is this not the one thing lacking in church life today? Is the world a 'wilderness' to us? We shall leave everything behind except our fellow pilgrims. May we prove the blessedness of true fellowship with them. May it be a means of preparing us for the glory to come.

1. HERCULES COLLINS
AND
THE ART OF PREACHING

When Oliver Cromwell died in 1658, some of the Puritan generals who had fought alongside him against the tyranny of the Stuarts during the Civil War (1642-1651) began to fear that anarchy was about to overtake English society. In a move that would have a profound impact down to the present day, they felt that they had no choice but to restore the monarchy in the person of Charles II (reigned 1660-1685). The generals, though, asked Charles to ensure that religious liberty would continue to exist as it had done during Cromwell's republic and Charles pledged himself to guarantee such freedom. Those who came to power with Charles, however, had no intention of allowing the Puritans this liberty. Over the next few years a repressive body of legislation, known as the Clarendon Code, was passed — having as its chief goal the destruction of the power base of the Puritan cause. The rulers of England were determined that never again would the Puritans exercise the sort of political power they had wielded during the 1640s and 1650s.

Nonconformists

The vast majority of the Puritans were subsequently forced out of the Church of England. They now found themselves to be all but second-class citizens. In fact, between 1660 and 1688, the Puritan cause was a church under the cross. The state actively harassed those outside the established church and imprisoned their leaders. Henceforth these Puritans (found primarily in three denominational groupings — Presbyterians, Congregationalist or Independents, and Calvinistic Baptists) would be collectively known in history as Nonconformists or Dissenters.

This book celebrates the memory and achievements of one strand of this dissenting body of men and women, namely the Calvinistic Baptists, 'of whom the world was not worthy'. The time period on which we shall focus is the 'long eighteenth century', from 1688/1689 (years that saw the establishment of the Glorious Revolution, bringing some genuine religious toleration to England and Wales) until 1815 (the end of the Napoleonic Wars).

We begin by looking at a figure whose life and ministry falls partly before the beginning of our time period, namely, Hercules Collins, the Calvinistic Baptist pastor of Wapping Street Baptist Church, London. Collins appears to have received little formal education. A keen interest in Christianity showed itself at an early age, which may indicate that his parents were Christians. If his parents were believers, the fact that they gave their son the name of a pagan Greek hero is curious, to say the least! Beyond this, though, nothing is known about his parents.

Pastor

There is some evidence that, by the mid-1670s, Hercules was a member of Petty France Particular Baptist Church in London. If so, he might have received some pastoral training in this congregation. On 23 March 1677, he was appointed pastor of the Wapping Particular Baptist Church in London, situated at that time between Broad

Street and Old Gravel Lane. God blessed his ministry and, ten years later, at the end of the summer of 1687, Collins moved the congregation to another London location. The congregation erected a new building for worship on James Street in Stepney. The boldness of the move — religious toleration had not yet been declared in England and Wales — displayed the vigorous leadership that Collins exercised both within his own church and in the larger Calvinistic Baptist community of London. Three years prior to this, in 1684, Collins had been imprisoned in Newgate under the provisions of the Five Mile Act (1665), which forbade Nonconformist preachers and pastors to live within 'five miles of any city or town or borough'. A defence of Nonconformity that Collins had penned two years earlier, *Some Reasons for Separation From the Communion of the Church of England, and the Unreasonableness of Persecution Upon that Account*, may well have been a factor in his imprisonment.

When toleration for Nonconformists did arrive in 1689, Collins was present at the national assembly of Particular Baptists that gave official sanction to a confessional document known as the *Second London Confession of Faith*. This would become the doctrinal standard for the British Calvinistic Baptist community well into the nineteenth century.

By the time that Collins died on 4 October 1702, he was probably preaching to a congregation of roughly 700 people. A funeral sermon preached by fellow London Baptist John Piggott, and later published, unfortunately contains the scantiest of biographical details. We thus know relatively little about Collins' life. He was buried in London's central Nonconformist burial ground, Bunhill Fields.

Theological writings

According to the early eighteenth-century Baptist historian Thomas Crosby (1683-c.1751), Collins did not enjoy the advantage of a learned education. Yet there is little doubt that he was well versed in theology. This is quite evident from a number of his publications. He published a Baptist version of the *Heidelberg Catechism* (1562) in 1680, which was entitled *An Orthodox Catechism*. And during the 1690s a steady stream of books and tracts issued from his pen. These publications dealt with a variety of subjects, such as divine sovereignty (*Mountains of Brass: or, A Discourse upon the Decrees of God*, 1690), believer's baptism (*Believer's Baptism from Heaven, and of Divine Institution*, 1691), and the death of infants (*Truth and Innocency Vindicated*, 1695).

In *Truth and Innocency Vindicated* Collins shows that he was not afraid of thinking differently from his Calvinistic Baptist contemporaries. The *Second London Confession of Faith* had asserted that 'elect infants, dying in infancy, are regenerated and saved by Christ through the Spirit' (10.3). Though he admitted that such 'secret things' are ultimately known only to God, Collins was 'inclined to believe all dying infants [are] in the Election and Covenant of Grace'.

The temple repaired

Collins' last work was *The Temple Repair'd* (1702), an eloquent plea for Calvinistic Baptist churches to serve as seminaries for aspiring pastors and preachers. In it, Collins tackled what appears to have been a controversial subject of his day. Should pastors 'study to declare God's mind'? There were evidently some in the Calvinistic Baptist community who 'contemptuously' spoke against such study, and believed (it seemed to Collins) that men 'were to preach by inspiration, as the Prophets and Apostles of old did'. Such individuals obviously regarded any preparation and study as fundamentally dishonouring to the Holy Spirit.

Collins unequivocally responds by emphasising what we would want to assert today — good preaching requires hard work and preparation. In his words, 'he doth the best work and the most work, that labours most in his study, with a dependence upon God for a blessing' (p.22). Collins was well aware that ultimately it is the Spirit who makes men preachers of the gospel — 'tho it be granted that human Literature is very useful for a Minister, yet it is not essentially necessary; but to have the Spirit of Christ to open the Word of Christ is essentially necessary' (p.19). But study is still vital, and 2 Timothy 2:15 was his salient refutation of the alternative view. The comparison of pastors with workmen in this text led Collins to declare, 'We should study to be good workmen, because our work is of the highest nature. Men that work among jewels and precious stones, ought to be very knowing of their business. A Minister's work is a great work, a holy work, a heavenly work' (p.22).

Sermons

Collins also gave instructions regarding the best way in which to shape a sermon. Attention first had to be given to the context of the verses being preached upon and difficult terms in the passage had to be explained. Then what the passage taught in terms of doctrine should be made fully clear and established by reference to parallel texts of Scripture. Finally, how the doctrinal teaching applied to the hearers' lives was to be set forth.

Among the various additional directions that the London pastor gave regarding preaching, were that the preacher's speech must be 'plain, as Paul's was. Not with enticing words of man's wisdom, but in demonstration of the Spirit, and of power (1 Corinthians 2:4). Use sound words that cannot be condemned. Rhetorical flashes are like painted glass in a window, that makes a great show but darkens the light ... The Prophets and Apostles generally spoke in the vulgar and common languages which the ordinary people understood: They did not only speak to the understanding of a King upon the throne, but to the understanding of the meanest subject' (p.28).

It was such 'sound words' that made many Calvinistic Baptist and Nonconformist pulpits of Collins' day places of light and fire — light that showed the way of salvation and fire that enflamed hearts with devotion to Christ.

2. WILLIAM MITCHEL
AND
ITINERANT EVANGELISM

According to some, the Calvinistic Baptists of the eighteenth century were in serious stagnation, even decline, for much of the century. This was the standard historical line on their condition before revival came to them from the late 1780s on into the nineteenth century. Increasingly, however, it is being recognised that such a reading of the primary sources of this era is far too simplistic. English Baptist historian Roger Hayden, for instance, has argued persuasively that the Calvinistic Baptists in the West Country managed to maintain a vibrant evangelical Calvinism throughout this period (Ph.D thesis, Keele University).

Itinerant evangelist

A good example of this spiritual vitality is William Mitchel (1662-1705) who evangelised tirelessly in the Pennines, from the Rossendale Valley in Lancashire to Rawdon in West Yorkshire. Mitchel was born at Heptonstall, not far from Hebden Bridge in Yorkshire. Nothing is really known about his upbringing. His conversion came at the age of nineteen after the death of a brother. Although he was genuinely converted, Mitchel later saw himself as something of a Jonah, as he sought to go into business as a clothier and become wealthy. But God frustrated his worldly ambitions and drew him out as a preacher of the gospel.

Within four years of his conversion, he began to work as an itinerant evangelist. His cousin, David Crosley (1669-1744), a stonemason turned preacher, tells us that Mitchel's aim in his preaching was to 'chiefly set forth the exceeding rich and free grace of the gospel, which toward him had been made so exceeding abundant'. At the same time, we are told that his Christian life was one of unwearied diligence in 'reading, meditation, and prayer'. Mitchel, Crosley and others travelled throughout the Pennines, often during the night so as to reach preaching venues in towns and villages by early morning. Crosley remembered the toil of walking 'many miles in dark nights and over dismal mountains'. But he also never forgot Mitchel's 'savoury and edifying' preaching that took place anywhere Mitchel could get an audience, 'on mountains, and in fields and woods'. Though Mitchel was not a polished speaker, crowds pressed to hear him.

Many came out of curiosity and some to scoff. But later, when their hearts and consciences had been moved by Mitchel's gospel preaching, they confessed, 'the Lord is with him of a truth'. On one occasion he delivered a sermon at Barnoldswick, Lancashire. Crosley later wrote, 'never did I feel such a living, nay, such a quickening, power' in Mitchel's preaching. It was 'like to a thunder-clap' that caused his heart to 'tremble and quake'.

Imprisoned

According to the Second Conventicle Act 1670 (part of the 'Clarendon Code' designed to break the spirit of the Nonconformists), what Mitchel was doing was illegal. The act forbade anyone over the age of sixteen from taking part in a religious assembly of more than five people unless it was sanctioned by the Church of England. The act gave wide powers to local magistrates and judges to 'suppresse [*sic*] and dissolve' such 'unlawfull [*sic*] meetings' and arrest whoever they wished to achieve this end.

Mitchel was twice arrested under this law during the reign of James II (reigned 1685-1688). On the first occasion he was treated with deliberate roughness and spent three months in jail at Goodshaw. On the second occasion he was arrested near Bradford and imprisoned for six months in York Castle. The enemies of the gospel who imprisoned Mitchel might have thought they were shutting him up in a dismal dungeon. To Mitchel, though, as he told his friends in a letter written from York in the spring of 1687, the dungeon was a veritable 'paradise, because the glorious presence of God is with me and the Spirit of glory and of God rests on

Heptonstall

me' (see 1 Peter 4:14). He had been given such a 'glorious sight of [God's] countenance, [and] bright splendour of his love', that he was quite willing to 'suffer afflictions with the people of God, and for his glorious truth'.

In a letter to a Daniel Moore during this same

imprisonment, Mitchel wrote that he had heard that James II had issued a Declaration of Indulgence, which pardoned all who had been imprisoned under the penal laws of the Clarendon Code. But he had yet to see it. Whatever the outcome, he told Moore, 'the Lord's will be done; let him order things as may stand with his glory'. This sentence speaks volumes about the frame of mind in which Mitchel had approached his time of imprisonment. He was God's servant. God would do with him as he sovereignly thought best. And Mitchel was quite content with that for, in his heart, he longed above all for his life to reflect God's glory.

Church-planting

After release from his second imprisonment in 1687, Mitchel did not hesitate to resume preaching throughout the valleys and towns of the Pennines. There is little doubt that Mitchel's evangelistic ministry was, at least in part, rooted in a love for perishing sinners. He told Richard Core, a fellow minister of the gospel, that the conversion of one poor soul is 'more worth than the whole world, yea than all the riches, honours, profits and pleasures of it, in which the whole world glories'. God was pleased to honour such a conviction, and through his ministry and that of Crosley twenty preaching stations were established in the Pennines. In time, the majority of these became Calvinistic Baptist churches.

Eventually Crosley moved on to preach further afield. He is described by one writer as having 'lacked the grace of settlement'. He ended up for a few years in London, where he became pastor of the Cripplegate church that Hanserd Knollys (1599-1691) had founded. Because of a fall into grave immorality, Crosley had to leave this church in 1709. By the following year he had made his way back to the north. It was long after Mitchel's death that Crosley regained his credibility and served as a pastor once more. Crosley's remarkable story has been superbly told by Baptist historian B. A. Ramsbottom in his booklet *The Puritan Samson: The Life of David Crosley 1669-1744* (1991).

Lasting fruit

Mitchel stayed in the north. Various letters of his have survived that show him shepherding the groups that had been gathered, answering doctrinal queries on such matters as election, fighting incipient Antinomianism — ever a bugbear for Calvinism — and enjoying fellowship in Christ with Congregationalists as well as Baptists. Running through all his labours was this keynote — to have 'less of man and more of Christ' and to 'have man laid low and more abased, and Christ exalted and more set up' (Letter to Friends at York, 13 July 1691).

In 1692 a meeting-house was erected in Bacup which became Michel's home church. Other meeting-houses would follow, some of which became important Baptist works in the years to come — Rodhill End, near Todmorden (1703); Cloughfold (1705); Gildersome (1707); Rawdon (1712). Mitchel died in 1705, before some of these churches were planted. His motivation, as he noted in one of his letters, was singular and clear; a desire for the good of souls and the glory of Christ.

As he wrote in one of his letters, concerning the groups of believers he sought to serve, 'What but entire love and a longing desire after the good of their souls could have induced me to have exposed myself as I have, in spending my time, wasting my health and strength, neglecting and slighting my family, and exposing myself to many reproaches ... so that surely my people and children for whom I have travailed in birth and pain, these many years, to see Christ brought forth in them, cannot think anything but pure love hath engaged me to what I have done upon their accounts and for them. As for honour and vainglory, I have neither sought it nor had it'.

I am indebted to the Local Studies Unit Archives, Manchester Central Library, for the use of the letters of William Mitchel. The letters are kept in the Papers of Dr William Farrer. Thanks are also due to David J. Woodruff of the Strict Baptist Historical Society who provided me with a copy of the letters.

3. THE CELEBRATED MRS ANNE DUTTON

While there were a number of first-class poetesses in the eighteenth century, female theological writers from that era are a distinct rarity. This makes the literary legacy of the Calvinistic Baptist Anne Dutton (1692-1765) extremely significant. Anne Dutton, née Williams, was born in Northampton to godly Congregationalist parents.

In her late teens she began attending an open-membership Baptist church in the town, pastored at the time by John Moore (d.1726). There, in her words, she found 'fat, green pastures, for Mr. Moore was a great doctrinal preacher'. As she went on to explain, 'the special advantage I received under his ministry was the establishment of my judgement in the doctrines of the gospel'. It was in this congregation that she was baptised as a believer.

Influenced by Hyper-Calvinists?

When she was twenty-two she married a Mr Cattell (his first name does not appear to be known) and moved to London. While there, she worshipped with the Calvinistic Baptist church that met at premises on Wood Street, Cripplegate. Founded by Hanserd Knollys, this work had known some rough times in the days immediately before Anne came to the church. David Crosley, pastor of the work from 1705 to 1709 and whom we have met in the previous chapter, had been disfellowshipped for drunkenness, unchaste conduct, and lying to the church about these matters when accused. Many years later, he would again know some usefulness in the Lord's work, but in the 1710s he had lost all credibility.

The sorrow and sense of betrayal and consternation in the church must have run deep. It was not until 1714 that the church succeeded in finding a new pastor. John Skepp (d. 1721), a member of the Cambridge Congregationalist Church of Joseph Hussey (1659-1726), was called that year to be the pastor.

Now Hussey is often seen as the father of Hyper-Calvinism. In his book *God's Operations of Grace but no Offers of Grace* (1707), he asserted that offering Christ indiscriminately to sinners is something that smacks of 'creature-co-operation and creature-concurrence' in the work of salvation. Skepp himself published but one book, and that posthumously. In his *Divine Energy: or The Efficacious Operations of the Spirit of God upon the Soul of Man* (1722) he appears to have followed Hussey's approach to evangelism. Thus it is sometimes argued that Anne Dutton's exposure to Hyper-Calvinism at a young age shaped her thinking for the rest of her life.

However, if Anne were deeply influenced by Hyper-Calvinism, it is curious to find her rejoicing in later years in the ministry of preachers like George Whitefield (1714-1770). If Anne did have Hyper-Calvinist leanings, they were not such as to prevent her from appreciating deeply what God was doing through men like Whitefield.

Skepp was an impressive preacher. The overall trend in the church during his ministry was one of growth. There were 179 members when he came as pastor in 1714. When he died in 1721, church membership had grown to 212.

And Anne delighted in his 'quickness of thought, aptness of expression, suitable affection, and a most agreeable delivery'.

Great Gransden

About 1720 Anne's life underwent a deep trial as her husband of only five or six years died. Returning to her family in Northampton, she was not long single. Her second marriage in the early 1720s was to Benjamin Dutton (1691-1747), a clothier who had studied for vocational ministry in various places, among them Glasgow University. Ministry took the couple to such towns as Whittlesey and Wisbech in Cambridgeshire, before leading them finally in 1731 to Great Gransden, Huntingdonshire.

Under Dutton's preaching the church flourished. On any given Sunday the congregation numbered between 250 and 350, of whom roughly 50 were members. This growth led to the building of a new meeting-house, which can still be seen in the village. Benjamin perished at sea, however, in 1747. He had gone to America to help raise funds to pay off the debt incurred in the building of the meeting-house. The ship on which he was returning foundered not far from the British coast.

Primitive piety

Widowed for the second time, Anne was to live another eighteen years. During that time 'the fame of her primitive piety' became known in evangelical circles on both sides of the Atlantic. The words cited are those of Baptist historian Joseph Ivimey (1773-1834) and referred to her New

Testament-like spirituality.

She had been writing for a number of years before Benjamin's demise. After his death a steady stream of tracts and treatises, collections of selected correspondence, and poems poured from her pen. Among her numerous correspondents were Howel Harris (1714-1773), Selina Hastings, Countess of Huntingdon (1707-1791), William Seward (1711-1740), George Whitefield, and Philip Doddridge (1702-1751).

Harris was convinced that the Lord had entrusted her 'with a talent of writing for him'. When Seward, an early Methodist preacher who was killed by a mob in Wales, read a letter from her in May 1739, he found it 'full of such comforts and direct answers to what I had been writing that it filled my eyes with tears of joy'. And Whitefield, who helped promote and publish Anne's writings, said after meeting her that 'her conversation is as weighty as her letters'.

Women writers

But she wrestled with whether it was biblical for her to be an authoress. In a tract entitled *A Letter to Such of the Servants of Christ, who May have any Scruple about the Lawfulness of PRINTING any Thing written by a Woman* (1743), she maintained that she wrote not for fame, but for 'only the glory of God, and the good of souls'. To those who might accuse her of violating 1 Timothy 2:12, she answered that her books were not intended to be read in a public setting of worship, which the text was designed to address. Rather, the instruction that her books gave was private, for they were read by believers in 'their own private houses'. She

asked those who opposed women writers to 'Imagine then
… when my books come to your house, that I am come to
give you a visit' and the opportunity to 'patiently attend'
to her 'infant lispings'.

What if some other women authors had used the press
for 'trifles'? Well, she answered, 'Shall none of that sex be
suffer'd to appear on Christ's side, to tell of the wonders of
his love, to seek the good of souls, and the advancement
of the Redeemer's interest?' She was not slow to critique
theological positions she felt erroneous. For instance, she
was a critic of John Wesley and his brand of evangelical
Arminianism, though her criticism was never abusive.
In addition to a number of letters to Wesley, she wrote a
booklet entitled *Letters to the Reverend Mr John Wesley
against Perfection as Not Attainable in this Life* (1743).

The Lord's Supper

One of her best pieces is a devotional study of the Lord's
Table, *Thoughts on the Lord's Supper, Relating to the Nature,
Subjects, and right Partaking of this Solemn Ordinance,*
which was published anonymously in 1748. It clearly reveals
Calvinistic Baptist piety at its best.

'Not a dram of new covenant-favour', she writes, 'was
to flow to the heirs of promise, but thro' the death of Jesus'.
This Christ-centredness and cross-centredness permeates
the entire treatise. To give but one further example: 'O
what a wondrous draught', she declares near the beginning
of the book, 'what a life-giving draught, in his own most
precious blood, doth God our Saviour, the Lord our lover,
give to dying sinners, to his beloved ones in this glorious
ordinance'.

For Anne and, one suspects, many of her fellow Baptist Dissenters, the Lord's Supper was a 'Royal banquet which infinite love hath prepared'. In fact, so high is her view of the Supper that she considers it 'the nearest approach to his glorious *Self*, that we can make in an ordinance-way on the earth, on this side [of] the presence of his glory in heaven'. This language may sound extravagant to some, but it reveals, I believe, something of the spiritual intensity that was available to Dissenting congregations in the mid-eighteenth century. In fact, one of the few negative effects of the Evangelical Revival may well be the way in which this spirituality was diluted in the rush to make churches primarily centres for evangelism.

A personal word

Though most of Anne's works survive now in only a few copies, they are well worth the effort of finding and reading. This writer can testify to the rich time he spent one October morning a few years ago on a train trip from Bedford to Gatwick Airport, reading some of Anne's letters. I had been given a copy of Anne's *Selections from Letters on Spiritual Subjects* (compiled and published in 1884) by Mr Nigel Pibworth of Biggleswade, and despite the press of the commuters that morning, I was gripped by the spirituality of her prose. Hopefully this brief introduction to her life will prompt a renewed appreciation of her legacy and spirituality.

The author would like to thank Mr Pibworth for the gift of a number of other sources that also helped immensely in the writing of this chapter.

4. ABRAHAM BOOTH
AND THE
ETHICS OF SLAVERY

What does it means to be human? This question is central to several critical ethical issues of our day. The resolution of the ethical dilemmas surrounding, for example, abor-

tion and genetic engineering cannot be found unless this question is answered. Although recent scientific advances have thrust such issues into the limelight, we are not the first generation to have to wrestle with them. The central ethical dilemma for eighteenth-century British society, on both sides of the Atlantic, was the slave trade and the owning of slaves.

The British slave trade

Great Britain's entry into the slave trade dates from 1562 when the Elizabethan adventurer Sir John Hawkins (1532-1595) took a shipload of three hundred West Africans and sold them to the Spanish in what is now the Dominican Republic. Elizabeth I (reigned 1558-1601) called his action 'detestable' and revulsion towards the slave trade appears to have prevailed among the English in the early seventeenth century. However, by the final decades of that century the British were taking around 45,000 slaves a year from the West African coast to the Caribbean and the American south. Altogether, they transported a total of some 3 million enslaved Africans to the New World.

The slave trade was driven by a desire for rapid economic development in Britain's New World colonies. The key event that drew Britain into this pernicious trade was the establishment of sugar plantations in the West Indies. In the first few decades of the seventeenth century, attempts to grow sugar in Bermuda and Virginia had failed. The turning-point came when the British settled Barbados in 1625. Within thirty years a thriving industry was established and sugar soon became the main export of the Caribbean islands. By 1730 the British were importing 100,000 hogshead of sugar annually to satisfy their 'sweet tooth'. The annual sugar revenue of Jamaica alone was estimated to be £1.6 million.

Abraham Booth

Evangelical Christians fiercely opposed the slave trade. British historian David Bebbington notes that 'arguments based on biblical principle did most to rouse anti-slavery feeling'. A particularly fine example of the biblical argument against slavery is found in a sermon by Abraham Booth (1734-1806) preached on 29 January 1792 at Prescot Street Baptist Church, London, where he was the pastor. The sermon was entitled *Commerce in the Human Species, and the Enslaving of Innocent Persons, inimical to the Laws of Moses and the Gospel of Christ*.

The son of a Nottinghamshire farmer, Booth became a stocking weaver in his teens. He had no formal schooling and taught himself to read and to write. His early Christian experience was among the General (i.e. Arminian) Baptists, but by 1768 he had undergone a complete revolution in his soteriology and had become a Calvinist. Not long afterwards he wrote *The Reign of Grace, from Its Rise to Its*

Consummation (1768), which Scottish theologian John Murray regarded as 'one of the most eloquent and moving expositions of the subject of divine grace in the English language'.

Unsullied kindliness

It was this book which led to his being called to Prescot Street Baptist Church in what was then a wealthy area of London, home to merchants and professional men. Pastoring this church was a challenge to one with so limited an education, but Booth more than rose to the challenge, mastering Greek, Latin and French. By the time of his death in 1806 he was one of the most trusted counsellors in the Calvinistic Baptist denomination. His congregation adored him for what contemporaries called his 'unsullied purity and kindliness'. One of them penned a most moving, though brief, tribute in the church minute book after his death: 'He sought not ours, but us'. This love for others is evident in his sermon against the slave trade.

Duty to adore our Maker

Commerce in the Human Species opens with the affirmation that every human being has a duty 'to adore our Almighty Maker, to confide in the Lord Redeemer, and to exercise genuine benevolence toward all mankind'. 'Genuine benevolence' needs to be shown by human beings in so far as they are 'social beings, surrounded with multitudes of [their] species'. In fact, Booth is convinced that the promotion of 'this cordial affection for our neighbours' is part of 'the great end of an evangelical ministry'. Booth goes on to emphasise that Evangelicalism is intimately tied up

with 'the exercise of moral justice, of benevolence, and of
humanity', and it is on this basis, and not that of promoting
civil and political liberty, that he is prepared to take a stand
against 'the stealing, purchasing, and enslaving of innocent
persons'.

Booth examines the Old Testament texts dealing with
slavery and recognises that Scripture does not condemn
every type of slavery. Jews, for example, could be sold
into servitude for such things as theft and insolvency. This
type of servitude is not at all comparable, Booth rightly
points out, to the life-long bondage of Africans in the West
Indies.

But the 'permission' that God gave to Israel to own
slaves was part and parcel of a civil code unique to Israel
and was only in effect while God was dealing with Israel
as a political entity. Once 'the Christian economy was
established, that prerogative ceased'. Booth must have been
well aware that there were those in the English-speaking
Reformed tradition who claimed that God had entered into
a similar sort of covenant with the English nation. But he
rightly rejects any such claim — 'the ancient distinction
between Jews and Gentiles being entirely abolished, by the
divine establishment of Christianity, those prerogatives
that were peculiar to Judaism and its professors do not
now exist'. Christianity is 'the religion of truth and of
justice, of benevolence and of peace'. The slave trade, on
the other hand, is 'unjust and cruel, barbarous and savage'.
Booth asserts that 'the rights of humanity' are the common
possession of the whole human species.

If the slave trade was lawful, he pointed out, then
Africans had the right to raid London, Bristol and Liverpool
(the three main English ports that had grown rich from

the traffic in human beings) and enslave free Britons! Imaginatively turning the tables, Booth puts his hearers in the shoes of the Africans, that they might develop a heart of benevolence towards them.

Benevolence

Not only is the slave trade condemned by the Old Testament, but is also inimical to the ethical teaching of Christ. Christians are to love even their enemies and do good to them that hate them (Luke 6:27). 'If our sovereign Lord requires benevolence and active love to our enemies', Booth reasons, surely he cannot require any less to those who are not our enemies. This would certainly include the Africans, who are unknown to the slave traders prior to their being enslaved.

The London Baptist minister also cites the so-called Golden Rule, Matthew 7:12 — 'all things whatsoever ye would that men should do to you, do ye even so to them' — to show that at the heart of gospel ethics is benevolence towards others. Booth knew that some would object that slavery was a central feature of the Graeco-Roman world, yet the New Testament nowhere condemns it. He rightly admits that there is no explicit condemnation of slavery in the New Testament. Yet neither is there any mention of gladiatorial games, which were 'extremely bloody and wicked'. The fact that slavery, like these Roman blood sports, violates the general moral principles of the Scriptures is sufficient warrant to argue as Booth does.

Actually, at the very beginning of the sermon, Booth had referred to a New Testament verse which does expressly condemn slavery and the slave trade. Paul's list of evildoers in 1 Timothy 1:9-10 includes 'menstealers'. Seeing this word as a reference to slave traders, Booth rightly suspects that this list is based on the Decalogue and that Paul is here referring to the Eighth Commandment.

Directions

The sermon concludes with directions as to how Christians can fight the slave trade. First of all, Booth exhorts prayer 'for the interposition of Providence to abolish the detestable traffic in man'. Africans were 'naturally as capable of being made the spiritual subjects of Jesus Christ' as Europeans, yet the slave trade hindered the propagation of Christianity among them. It was only right, therefore, that in praying for 'the enlargement of our Lord's visible kingdom among men', Christians should pray for its abolition. Moreover, Booth believed that Christians should pray for 'the gradual emancipation' of the existing West Indian slaves.

Booth also emphasised that there should be 'prudent, peaceable, and steady efforts, in order to procure the total abolition of that criminal traffic, and of the cruel slavery consequent upon it'. He urged Christians to give financial support to the Society for the Abolition of the African Slave Trade, with which the great evangelical politician William Wilberforce was involved. Booth did not live to see the end of the British slave trade in 1807 nor the emancipation of the slaves in 1833. Yet his sermon witnesses to the growing tide of revulsion at the traffic in human souls and the determination of Evangelicals to pray it out of existence. May God give us grace to be worthy heirs of the social piety of men like Abraham Booth!

5. JOHN RYLAND JR.
AND
THE BRISTOL ACADEMY

In September 1753 Samuel Davies (1723-1761), a Presbyterian minister from Virginia, left his home for Great Britain on what would turn out to be an arduous though highly successful expedition His purpose was to raise funding for the fledgling College of New Jersey (later to be renamed Princeton University). He was gone for a total of eighteen months, and met a number of key British Evangelicals and churchmen, among them the leading Baptist theologian of the era, John Gill (1697-1771) — whom he described as 'the celebrated Baptist minister'.

Davies paid a visit to Gill on 30 January 1754 and found him 'a serious, grave little man'. Gill was quite willing to lend his support to the College, but he told Davies not to expect much from the English Baptists as a whole — 'in general', he said, the Baptists 'were unhappily ignorant of the importance of learning'.

Bristol Baptist College

Early years

A striking exception to John Gill's censure of his fellow Baptists was his friend John Collett Ryland (1723-1792), who had a voracious appetite for learning. For much of his life J. C. Ryland was pastor of College Lane Baptist Church, Northampton, and one of the leading Calvinistic Baptist lights of the eighteenth century. He seems to have sought to stimulate an appetite for books and learning in his children, in particular, his namesake John Ryland Jr. (1753-1825).

For instance, around 1758 the younger Ryland had been so fascinated by watching his father teach Hebrew to some boys that he apparently asked if he could learn Hebrew as well. So it was that before the age of six he was able to read the twenty-third Psalm in Hebrew! In fact, he remembered reading it to the notable evangelical author James Hervey (1714-1758) who was a close friend of his father. Ryland was something of a precocious child but he also genuinely loved study from an early age. He recalled that as a young child he 'was fond of reading, and generally preferred that employment to play'. In the father's Diary for 28 August 1764 there is the following remarkable entry:

'John is now eleven years and seven months old; he has read Genesis in Hebrew five times through; he read through the Greek Testament before nine years old. He can read Horace and Virgil. He has read through Telemachus in French! He has read through Pope's *Homer*, in eleven volumes; read Dryden's *Virgil*, in three volumes. He has read Rollin's ancient history, ten volumes 8vo. And he knows the Pagan mythology surprisingly'. H. Wheeler Robinson commented on this diary entry, 'There is more than paternal pride in those words; there is the sense that he is giving to his boy that which he was once so eager to win for himself'.

The elder Ryland's piety also influenced his son. Though at times quite eccentric, the father was an ardent lover of the Lord Jesus. 'What a glory to be connected with all the infinite good in Christ', he wrote on one occasion in a small piece enumerating encouragements to pray. Thus, devotion and learning were interwoven early on in the life of the younger Ryland.

Ministry in Northampton and friendships

Ryland experienced conversion and baptism in 1767. In May 1770 he spoke for the first time before the church. His sermon was based on Jeremiah 31:8-9. The Northampton church formally recognized his gift for preaching in March 1771. He was but eighteen years old. Many years later he could say that he had 'had very few silent Sabbaths since'.

In 1781 Ryland was invited by College Lane to become co-pastor with his father. When his father moved five years later to Enfield, near London, Ryland became the sole pastor. During his early years of ministry Ryland received much solid and judicious advice and encouragement from John Newton (1725-1807), the Anglican Evangelical. Ryland's friendship with Newton began a few years after the latter had become curate at the parish church in Olney in 1764, and it lasted until Newton's death in 1807. The year before Ryland's own death in 1825, he summed up his friendship with Newton in this way; 'Mr Newton invited me to visit him at Olney in 1768; and from thence to his death, I always esteemed him, and Mr Hall of Arnsby … as my wisest and most faithful counsellors, in all difficulties'.

One gets a good understanding of the way that Newton, ever the mentor of younger pastors, helped Ryland when one ponders the following extracts of a letter he sent to Ryland when Ryland's first wife Betsy was on the verge of death. It was written on 23 January 1787.

'My dear friend, I feel, but I do not fear, for you. The God whom thou servest he can support and deliver you. He is all sufficient, and his promise is sure. Plenty of advice is at hand, but I dare not offer you much in this way. You are in the heat of a trial; I am at present in quiet. It would be easy for me to press patience and resignation upon you, and to remind you that a pardoned sinner ought never to complain. You could speak the same language to me, if I were in your case, and you were at ease. Yet though we may and ought to compassionate one another under our various trials, and to speak with tenderness where the heart is wounded, there are truths which, if trouble hides them from our view, it is the office of a friend to recall them. You and I are ministers. As such, how often have we commended the gospel as the το εν ['the one thing' that is needed], affording those who truly receive it, a balm for every wound, a cordial for every care!

'How often have we told our hearers, that our all-sufficient and faithful Lord can and will make good every want and loss! How often have we spoken of the light of his countenance as a full compensation for every suffering, and of the trials of the present life as not worthy to be compared with the exceeding abundant and eternal weight of glory to which they are leading! We must not therefore wonder, if we are sometimes called to exemplify the power of what we have said, and to show our people that we have not set before them unfelt truths, which we have learnt from books and men only. You are now in a post of honour, and many eyes are upon you. May the Lord enable you to glorify *him*, and to encourage *them*, by your exemplary submission to his will!

'You are doubtless allowed to pour out your heart before

him, and even to pray for Mrs Ryland's recovery, and I will join with you so far as I dare … I pray for her, that he may enable her quietly and cheerfully to commit herself into his hands; and I pray for you, that you may do the same. You may be assured he will not try you beyond what he will enable you to bear. If it be for your good, especially for your chief good, *his glory*, she shall recover; he will restore her, though a hundred physicians had given her up. If otherwise, I doubt not but he will help you to say, Thy will be done. And hereafter you shall see that his will was best … Accept this hasty line as a token of my sympathy. I was not willing to wait till I could find more leisure. May the Lord bless you both. And may we all so weep as becomes those who expect, ere long, to have all our tears wiped away. I am sincerely and affectionately yours, John Newton'.

Reading Jonathan Ewdards

During his early ministerial experience Ryland also read deeply in the writings of Jonathan Edwards (1703-1758). Indeed, after the Scriptures, Edwards' writings exerted the strongest theological influence on Ryland. As Ryland declared in a letter to his fellow Baptist Joseph Kinghorn (1766-1832), 'Were I forced to part with all mere human compositions but three, Edwards's *Life of Brainerd,* his *Treatise on Religious Affections*, and [Joseph] Bellamy's *True Religion Delineated* … would be the last I should let go'. And in a postscript to his funeral sermon for his closest friend Andrew Fuller (1754-1815) he stated:

'If I knew I should be with … Fuller tomorrow, instead of regretting that I had endeavoured to promote that religion delineated by Jonathan Edwards in his *Treatise*

on Religious Affections and in his *Life of David Brainerd*,
I would recommend his writings ... with the last effort I
could make to guide a pen'.

The 'religion delineated by Jonathan Edwards' was
devoted to a scholarly and contemporary defence of
Calvinistic convictions, and to tracing the work of the Spirit
in corporate revival and individual renewal. This twin
commitment that was characteristic of Edwards' theological
reflection, also provided both shape and substance for
Ryland's own theology. Ryland had enormous respect for
Edwards whom he considered 'one of the greatest and best
of men' in his personal life, and whom he esteemed as 'the
most skilful and successful opposer' of religious fanaticism
and 'one of the ablest defenders of the distinguishing
doctrines of Revelation'. Ryland also carried on an extensive
correspondence with a number of Edwardsean divines in
New England — men such as Jonathan Edwards, Jr., Samuel
Hopkins and Timothy Dwight.

Teaching in Bristol

In 1793 Ryland moved to Bristol where, until his death
in 1825, he was the pastor of Broadmead Church and the
principal of Bristol Baptist Academy. The year before he
moved to Bristol, Ryland played a key role in founding what
would come to be called the Baptist Missionary Society. His
friend Andrew Fuller was the first secretary of this society,
and when Fuller died in 1815 Ryland succeeded him.

An outstanding Hebrew scholar and solid preacher,
Ryland exercised a significant influence on the lives of the
two hundred or so students who studied at Bristol during
his time as principal. The student body was never huge at

any one time — in 1816 for example, there were 22 students studying at the school. Yet, the majority of them went on to become Baptist pastors and missionaries, imbued with Ryland's evangelical Calvinism and commitment to revival.

Over time, Ryland became one of the respected pillars of Calvinistic Baptist life in England. On one occasion, when his successor Robert Hall (1764-1831) was told something he regarded as incredible, Hall asked on whose authority the report was based. When he was told that the source was Ryland, he replied, 'Did Ryland say so, Sir? Then it is true, Sir; for I would as soon receive his testimony as the affidavit of seven archangels'.

Hymns

Finally, brief mention should be made of the fact that, in addition to numerous published sermons, Ryland also wrote a number of hymns. His earliest literary pieces had actually been poems. Two of his hymns especially remain in circulation: *Sovereign Ruler of the Skies* and *O Lord, I would delight in Thee*. They are not high-flying, soaring pieces of hymnody, but they well convey what Ryland deemed important in the Christian life. Of those, the most important was seeking God, as he wrote in the hymn named above:

O Lord, I would delight in thee,
And on thy care depend;
To thee in every trouble flee,
My best, my only Friend.

Map of India

Himalayan Mountains

Bengal

Serampore

Calcutta

Bay of Bengal

Indian Ocean

6. JOHN THOMAS
AND THE
MISSION TO INDIA

Often forgotten, John Thomas (1757-1801) accompanied William Carey (1761-1834) as a missionary to India in 1793. The Baptist historian Ernest Payne once said of him, 'no stranger figure can ever have played an influential role in missionary history'. His friends, like Carey and Andrew Fuller, noted that his character had a number of glaring faults — he was prone to extreme mood swings, was sometimes easily angered, had little money-sense, and was given to impatience.

William Carey, though, had been convinced that Thomas was 'a man of great closet piety', very compassionate in his dealings with the poor in India, and indefatigable in teaching those who were seeking for truth. Fuller, for his part, had no doubt that Thomas' style of preaching was well suited to India — 'a lively, metaphorical, and pointed address on divine subjects, dictated by the circumstances of the moment, and maintained amidst the interruptions and contradictions of a heathen audience'.

Christ's benefits

Thomas came from a Baptist home in Fairford, Gloucestershire, where his father was a deacon in what was a sturdy Baptist community. Thomas was not

found by Christ, however, until he was in London, and
sat under the preaching of Samuel Stennet (1727-1795),
pastor of Little Wild Street Baptist Church. His conversion
came in 1781. In his diary, Thomas describes how he spent
'many days and nights ... in the enjoyment of believing
that Christ had died for me in particular. Me, me, so
insignificant, so worthless! That such a one as I should be
a partaker of his benefits! — this thought attended me for
many days, wherever I was. I had many tears of joy and
gladness'. Subsequent Christian experience, though, was for
Thomas a series of emotional ups and downs, the result of
his impulsive and imprudent nature. And yet, burning in
his heart was an unquenchable passion to see Christ exalted
among the nations.

Concern for India

Thomas had trained as a doctor at Westminster Hospital,
London. When he ran into financial difficulties he decided
to take the position of surgeon on one of the ships of the
East India Company. During his second voyage to India in
1786 he became friends with Charles Grant (1746-1823), an
Anglican Evangelical who was on the Board of Trade of this
powerful company and was based in Calcutta. Grant helped
him start a missionary enterprise in Bengal, where Thomas
began to learn Bengali and to translate the Scriptures into
that tongue. He also made some headway in learning
Sanskrit. He was deeply moved by the wretchedness, both
spiritual and material, of many of the Indian people, and
longed to alleviate it.

By 1790, for a variety of reasons (not the least of
which were Thomas' increasing financial indebtedness and
mercurial temper), the friendship between Thomas and

Grant soured; so much so that Grant, in the later words of Carey, 'cut off all [Thomas'] supplies, and left him to shift for himself in a foreign land'. Thomas, still deep in debt, had to return to England in the early months of 1792 to secure funds to undergird his missionary work in Bengal. He also hoped to find, if at all possible, a like-minded companion for the work in India. Almost as soon as the ship had made landfall in England on 8 July, Thomas got in touch with Samuel Stennett and Abraham Booth, two of the leading Baptist pastors in London, informing them of his desire with regard to a mission to India. It was Booth who put Thomas into contact with Carey.

Baptist Missionary Society

Providentially, Thomas had arrived in England just as a group of Baptists from the Midlands were about to form a missionary society. During the late 1780s and early 1790s, Carey had been gazing upon wider spiritual horizons than the fields of his native Northamptonshire. He was increasingly gripped by the desperate

Andrew Fuller

spiritual plight of those who lived in countries utterly devoid of Christian witness. Many of them had no written language; certainly none of them had the Scriptures in their own tongues; and there were neither local churches nor resident ministers to share with them the good news of God's salvation. 'Pity, therefore, humanity and, much more, Christianity', Carey wrote in a book published in 1792, calling 'loudly for every possible exertion to introduce the gospel amongst them'.

Equally persuaded of the importance of cross-cultural missions were fourteen men, including Fuller, John Ryland Jr. and John Sutcliff (1752-1814). They met in the back parlour of the home of Martha Wallis (d. 1812), the widow of a deacon of Kettering Baptist Church, Northamptonshire, on 2 October 1792 — to form what would in time be called the Baptist Missionary Society. In its early days, however, it was called 'The Particular Baptist Society for propagating the Gospel amongst the Heathen'. Thomas met up with these men in January 1793, and within a short period of time he and William Carey became the society's first missionary appointees.

Depression

Thomas spent the final eight years of his life in India. His unstable character reasserted itself, and he often alternated, in Ernest Payne's words, between 'intense excitability and deep depression'. His friends 'either saw him full of cheerful and active love', wrote Fuller, 'or his hands hanging down as if he had no hope'. During one of Thomas' times of depression, Fuller sought to help him in a letter he wrote in May 1796:

'How could I weep on your account. Nay, before I write any more, I will go aside, and weep and pray for you, to him who alone can deliver your soul from death and keep your feet from falling. My dear Brother, it has afforded me some consolation, while pleading with God on your behalf, that his help could fly swifter than this letter. O that before this arrives you may be delivered from the horrible pit!'

Carey eventually established himself and his family in Mudnabati, about 300 miles north of Calcutta. Thomas lived seventeen miles away at Mypaldighi. There Thomas' house became, in the words of his nineteenth-century biographer C. B. Lewis, 'the place of resort for all the sick and poor in the district around ... The generous assistance of the compassionate missionary was never refused in any case of distress'. In a letter that Thomas wrote during his time at Mypaldighi, he refers to this ministry: 'I have patients from all parts, all poor and costly, but some of my sweetest moments are spent in giving them relief'. His most famous patient would be Krishna Pal (1764-1822), the first native Indian to be reached for Christ by the Baptist mission.

Krishna Pal

By this time, Thomas had relocated with Carey to Serampore, fourteen miles north of Calcutta on the west bank of the Hooghly River. It was here that the heart of the mission would henceforth remain.

Pal, a carpenter, had heard the gospel through Moravian missionaries some time before, but it had had little impact. On 26 November 1800 he fell and dislocated his shoulder. Having heard that there was a doctor at Serampore, the Indian carpenter sought out Thomas — who set Krishna Pal's dislocated arm and also took the opportunity to share the gospel with him. The Indian returned a few days later to tell Thomas and the other Baptist missionaries that he knew himself to be 'a very great sinner'. But he had confessed his sins and had 'obtained', he told them, the 'righteousness of Jesus Christ; and I am free'. Pal declared himself ready to break caste and be baptised. He was subsequently baptised by Carey on Sunday 28 December 1800 in the Hooghly River. William Ward, Carey's missionary co-worker, wrote thus in his diary of this baptism: 'The chain of the caste is broken; who shall mend it?'

Fitting

The joy of Krishna Pal's conversion and baptism was among the last Thomas enjoyed in this world. Not long after Pal's baptism, Thomas suffered a major mental breakdown. The strain of missionary work and his medical practice were largely responsible. By October 1801 he lay dying at the home of Ignatius Fernandez (1757-1831). Thomas had been instrumental in the conversion of Fernandez, who had been raised in a Portuguese Roman Catholic home in Macao, and whose parents had wanted him to become a priest. Fernandez lived at Dinajpur in North Bengal, and it was there on 13 October 1801 that Thomas died.

It is fitting to remember Thomas, for he has often been judged badly by history and historians. In one recent account of Carey's life all that is stated of Thomas is that he 'squandered' all the money the two men brought to India. In this case, older studies are much more reliable. One of the earliest chroniclers of the Baptist Missionary Society wrote that although Thomas 'was not without his failings, yet his peculiar talents, his intense, though irregular, spirituality, and his constant attachment to that beloved object, the conversion of the heathen, will render his memory dear as long as the mission endures'.

7. COXE FEARY AND THE AWAKENING IN BLUNTISHAM

Coxe Feary (1759-1822) sustained a long pastorate in the village of Bluntisham, about fifteen miles north of Cambridge, England. He was raised in the Church of England, but during his teens became dissatisfied with the irreligious conduct of worshippers at the parish church. He considered attending a Baptist church in a nearby village — perhaps the work at Needingworth, which had been founded in 1767. But he found the church consisted of 'narrow-minded' hyper-Calvinists, who pronounced 'destruction on all who did not believe their creed'. For a while he attended a Quaker congregation in Earith, another nearby village, because their views accorded with his belief in the freedom of the human will and the saving merit of good works.

Conversion

In 1780 he read James Hervey's *Theron and Aspasio* (1755), a massive defence of Calvinism. The book greatly challenged Feary's religious notions and he was deeply disturbed by its arguments. Offended, he put the book down without finishing it. But two years later he felt constrained to pick it up again and give it a fair hearing. The result was his glorious conversion. He was seized with a passion for the

salvation of the lost in his village. For instance, he wrote
the following plain words to a neighbour in 1783:

'I must beg you to attend to the Scriptures, and to pray
to God that he may enlighten your mind by his Holy Spirit,
that you may see the gracious privileges contained therein.
They, my friend, are the only rule for us to walk by — they
testify of Christ [and] point him out as the only procuring
cause of a sinner's acceptance with God, and his enjoyment
of eternal felicity. He hath made peace through the blood
of his cross, and through that blood we have redemption.
It is with regret of mind, my friend, that I think of your
carelessness, for I have a great desire for your everlasting
welfare, which has been my chief motive for writing to you.
Therefore, examine yourself impartially — consider how
your affairs stand with God, and see if you have an interest
in the merits of Christ; for if you have not (I dare not flatter
you) you are in a state of death. I hope, therefore, you will
say, "What must I do to be saved". I shall reply, "Believe on
the Lord Jesus Christ, and you shall be saved".'

Awakening

The awakening in Bluntisham took place during 1784-1785.
By 1784 Feary was sitting under the evangelical preaching
of Henry Venn (1724-1797) at Yelling, about ten miles
away. That same year he came across the works of George
Whitefield (1714-1770) in a bookshop in St Ives. What is
amazing is that he had never heard of Whitefield or his
remarkable ministry. So taken was he with the sermons of
the great evangelist that, the very same evening, he read one
of them — 'What think ye of Christ?' — aloud to a small
gathering of shepherds and farm labourers in his house.

It must have made an impact, for the following evening a man of means in the village, a certain John Kent, arrived with several others requesting Feary to read another sermon. Flustered by the group, and afraid of being considered 'a Methodist preacher', Feary refused. But the impromptu congregation would not take no for an answer and Feary relented. A poor woman was so deeply moved by Whitefield's words that she urged Feary to read yet a third time at her house the following evening. Feary agreed on the condition that she would tell no one. But the thing could not be hid. When he arrived at the house it was packed with neighbours.

Feary continued reading sermons in that woman's home throughout the winter of 1784-1785. In the spring of 1785 they had to move to a larger home to accommodate the numbers attending. A genuine spiritual awakening gripped the village, as many were moved to ask that old, but utterly vital, question, 'What must I do to be saved?' This work of revival laid the foundation of the Calvinistic Baptist work in Bluntisham.

Eventually, Feary ran out of sermons to read. So it was that he ventured to expound a section of Scripture himself. A barn had been fitted out for the congregation by John Kent and, on 28 December 1786, Coxe Feary and twenty-five other believers joined together to form a Congregationalist church. They came from a number of the surrounding villages, including Colne, Somersham, and Woodhurst. Feary was chosen as their first pastor.

Becoming Baptist

Over the next few years, friendship with Robert Robinson

(1735-1790), the well-known Baptist of Cambridge and author of the hymn *Come, Thou fount of every blessing*, led to Feary's embracing Baptist views. But it may also have been this friendship which led Feary to imbibe deistic ideas, for in his final years Robinson did not maintain a firm grasp on orthodox doctrines. Feary recalled this period of his life (the early 1790s) thus:

'I appeared infatuated with a desire of wild speculations which ... soon produced a kind of scepticism, which led me to look on all Christian experience as enthusiasm [fanaticism] and was ready to treat it with the utmost contempt, as cant and hypocrisy. This brought a damp upon my soul, chilled my affections for God, and love for the souls of my people. In this state of mind, my devotional exercises were, at times, very formal and flat. Preaching became dry, and I believe very uninteresting. No conversation suited me, but that which turned upon politics or theological controversy. In short, I appeared to myself to be making rapid strides to Infidelity and Deism'.

It is amazing that a man who had known revival at the beginning of his ministry should sink to such depths! But by the close of 1791 Feary had become alarmed at what was happening to him. He was brought, he said, 'to lament my case before God, who very justly might have given me up to strong delusions to believe a lie, as a sure sign of future destruction. But, adored be his holy name, he has caused the riches of his grace to be manifested in me, the chief of sinners, by bringing me back to his fold again. I am, beyond the shadow of doubt, confident, that salvation is entirely of grace, and that Jehovah will have mercy because he will have mercy'.

A useful preacher

Eighteenth-century Calvinistic Baptists, like many of their fellow Dissenters, regarded preaching as the pre-eminent aspect of public worship. But not everything that went by the name of preaching pleased them. They wanted plainness and simplicity in preaching.

We have already noted in Chapter 1 the words of Hercules Collins who spoke about preaching thus: 'Rhetorical flashes are like painted glass in a window, that makes a great show, but darkens the light ... The Prophets and Apostles generally spoke in the vulgar and common languages which the ordinary people understood. They did not only speak to the understanding of a king upon the throne, but to the understanding of the meanest subject'.

Writing in the autumn of 1802 to a friend studying at the Bristol Baptist Academy (the only Baptist seminary in England at the time) Feary counselled, 'I hope you make a point of studying two sermons every week, that you disuse your notes as much as possible in the pulpit, and that you constantly aim to be the *useful*, more than the *refined*, preacher'. Feary explained that he was not advocating the use of 'vulgar' speech or common slang in sermons. Rather, he wanted his friend 'to commend [himself] to every man's conscience in the sight of God, and to the understanding of [his] hearers'. In other words, his sermons should be easily understood by all his hearers, so that he would be a 'useful' preacher and 'an able minister of the New Testament'.

Permanent change

Such a minister was Feary. After his death in 1822, Newton

Bosworth (1776-1848), a well-known Baptist of the era who eventually emigrated to Canada, said of him:

'Mr Feary was in many respects, an extraordinary man. The moral reformation which, by the blessing of God, he effected in his native village, and its neighbourhood, and which must have afforded him, in the retrospect, unspeakable delight, is an event to which under all its circumstances not many parallel cases can be adduced. Without education, except in the slightest elements of it … he produced a most remarkable and permanent change in a great part of the population around him; commencing his labours without a single follower, continuing them, with an ardent, yet well-tempered zeal, amidst alternate hopes and fears, successes and discouragements, and ending by the formation of a flourishing church and congregation — the latter amounting to seven or eight hundred persons. If, as Scriptures assure us, "he that winneth souls is wise", Coxe Feary's reputation as a wise man cannot be disputed'.

8. THE SERAPHIC PEARCE

Though scarcely known today, Samuel Pearce was renowned for the depth of his spirituality and the anointing that attended his preaching. William Jay (1769-1853), a contemporary who exercised an influential ministry in Bath, remarked, 'When I have endeavoured to form an image of our Lord as a preacher, Pearce has oftener presented himself to my mind than any other ... [he had a] mildness and tenderness ... [a] peculiar unction'. Historians David Bogue and James Bennett made similar remarks.

When he preached, they said, 'the most careless were attentive, the most prejudiced became favourable, and the coldest felt that, in spite of themselves, they began to kindle'. But it was when he prayed in public, they remarked, that Pearce's spiritual ardour was most apparent: 'The most devout were so elevated beyond their former heights, that they said, "We scarcely ever seemed to pray before". He was rightly called 'the seraphic Pearce'.

Formative years

Pearce was born in Plymouth on 20 July 1766 to devout Baptist parents. His mother died when he was an infant, and he was raised by his godly father, William Pearce (d. 1805) and an equally pious grandfather.

He would also have known the nurture of the 'sturdy

Baptist community' of Plymouth, whose history reached back well into the seventeenth century. The heritage of these Baptists is seen in the character of one of their early ministers, Abraham Cheare (d. 1668). During 1660-1688, a time of great persecution for all Christians outside the Church of England, Cheare was arrested, cruelly treated and imprisoned on Drake's Island in Plymouth Sound.

Fearful that some of his flock might compromise their Baptist convictions to avoid persecution, he wrote letters to his church during his imprisonment. In one of them he cites the Puritan author Jeremiah Burroughs (c.1599-1646): 'standing in the gap is more dangerous and troubelsom [*sic*] than getting behind the hedge, [for] there you may be more secure and under the wind; but it's best to be ... where God looks for a man'. Cheare was one who 'stood in the gap', dying in 1668 while still imprisoned for his Baptist convictions.

In his teens, however, Pearce spurned the rich heritage of his godly home and community. 'Several vicious school-fellows' became close friends and he pursued 'wicked inclinations'. But God had better plans for his life. In the summer of 1782, Isaiah Birt (1758-1837) came to preach in the Plymouth meeting-house. The Spirit of God drove Birt's words home to Pearce's heart. The change in Pearce from 'a state of death in trespasses and sins' to a 'life in a dear dying Redeemer' was sudden but real and lasting. Pearce was conscious of the Spirit's witness in his heart that he was a child of God, and of being 'filled with peace and joy unspeakable'. A year or so later, on his seventeenth birthday, he was baptised and joined the Plymouth congregation. The church soon perceived that he had been endowed with the gifts of pastoral ministry. So, in November 1785, when he was only 19 and apprenticed to his silversmith father, Pearce was called to engage in the ministry of the Word.

Training and call

From August 1786 to May 1789 Pearce attended the Bristol Baptist Academy, the only institution in Great Britain training ministers for the Calvinistic Baptist denomination. He was ever grateful for the benefits afforded by this period of study. He had, for example, the privilege of studying under Caleb Evans (1737-1791), the Principal of the Academy, and Robert Hall, Jr. (1764-1831). The latter was a reputed genius destined to become one of the great preachers of the early 19th century. Students had opportunities to preach. Years later Pearce recalled going to preach to the colliers of Coleford, Gloucestershire. Standing on a three-legged stool in a hut, he directed thirty or forty of these miners to 'the Lamb of God which taketh away the sin of the world'. 'Such an unction from above' attended his preaching that day that his hearers were 'melted into tears' and he too, 'weeping among them, could scarcely speak ...'

Early in 1789 Pearce accepted a call to serve a year's probation as pastor of Cannon Street Baptist Church in Birmingham. He had supplied the pulpit there during the previous summer and the Christmas vacation. Impressed by Pearce's evangelistic zeal — people were saved on both occasions — and his ability to edify God's people, the church sent their request in February 1789. Five weeks later Pearce consented and, his studies finished, he joined them in June. The following year he was formally called to be the pastor of what would turn out to be his only pastoral charge. In his letter of acceptance, dated 18 July 1790, he expressed his hope that the union between pastor and church would 'be for God's glory, for the good of precious souls, for your prosperity as a Church, and for my prosperity as your minister'. He put 'God's glory' in first place. If anything set the tone of his ministry it was this desire to see God glorified in his life and labours.

Fruitfulness

His ministry at Cannon Street occupied ten all-too-brief years, but they were years of great fruitfulness. No fewer than 335 were baptised and received into membership during this period. This does not include those converted under his preaching who, for one reason or another, did not join his church. A Sunday school was started in 1795 and soon had some 1200 scholars.

At the heart of his preaching and spirituality was that key-note of Evangelicalism — the mercy of God displayed in the cross of Christ. Writing one Sunday afternoon to William Summers, a friend residing in London, Pearce said that he had for his sermon that evening 'the best subject of all in the Bible, Ephesians i.7 — Redemption! How welcome to the captive! Forgiveness! How delightful to the guilty! Grace! How pleasant to the heart of a saved sinner!' Christ's atoning death for sinners, he continued, is 'the leading truth in the NT ... a doctrine I cannot but venerate; and to the Author of such a redemption my whole soul labours to exhaust itself in praise'.

In his final letter to his congregation, written on 31 May 1799, he reminded them that the gospel which he had preached among them for ten years, and in which he urged them to stand fast, was 'the gospel of the grace of God; the gospel of free, full, everlasting salvation, founded on the sufferings and death of God manifest in the flesh'.

Struggles and convictions

People called Pearce 'silver-tongued' because of the intensity and power of his preaching. But there were times when preaching was a real struggle for him. Writing to William Carey in 1796, he told the Baptist missionary: 'At some times, I question whether I ever knew the grace of God in truth; and at others I hesitate on the most important points of Christian faith ... When I am preparing for the pulpit, I fear I am going to avow fables for facts and doctrines of men for the truths of God. In conversation I am obliged to be silent, lest my tongue should belie my heart. In prayer I know not what to say, and at times think prayer altogether useless. Yet I cannot wholly surrender my hope, or my profession. Three things I find, above all others, tend to my preservation. First, a recollection of time when, at once, I was brought to abandon the practice of sins which the fear of damnation could never bring me to relinquish before. Surely, I say, this must be the finger of God, according to the Scripture doctrine of regeneration. Second, I feel such a consciousness of guilt that nothing but the gospel scheme can satisfy my mind respecting the hope of salvation. And, thirdly, I see that what true devotion does appear in the world, seems only to be found among those to whom Christ is precious'.

Sovereign love

A handful of his sermons were published, as well as

the circular letter he drew up for the Midland Baptist Association in 1795 entitled *Doctrine of Salvation by Free Grace Alone*. A good perspective on his thought may be found in the following extract from this letter:

'We renounce everything in point of our acceptance with God but his free grace alone which justifies the ungodly, still treading in the steps of our venerable forefathers, the compilers of the Baptist Confession of Faith … In this point do all the other lines of our confession meet. For if it be admitted that justification is an act of free grace in God without any respect to the merit or demerit of the person justified; then the doctrines of Jehovah's sovereign love in choosing to himself a people from before the foundation of the world, his sending his Son to expiate *their* guilt, his effectual operations upon *their* hearts, and his perfecting the work he has begun in them until those whom he justifies he also glorifies, will be embraced as necessary parts of the glorious scheme of our salvation'.

Evangelistic spirituality

A leading characteristic of Pearce's spirituality, already noted, was his continual focus on the cross of Christ. 'Christ crucified', wrote his good friend and biographer Andrew Fuller, 'was his darling theme, from first to last'.

Another prominent feature of his spirituality was a passion for the salvation of his fellow men. On a preaching trip to Wales in July 1792, for instance, he wrote to his wife Sarah about the lovely countryside: 'every pleasant scene which opened to us on our way (and they were very numerous) lost half its beauty because my lovely Sarah was not present to partake its pleasures with me'. But, he added, 'to see the Country was not the immediate object of my visiting Wales — I came to preach the gospel — to tell poor sinners of the dear Lord Jesus — to endeavour to restore the children of misery to the pious pleasures of divine enjoyment'. This passion is strikingly revealed in the following incident.

In May 1794 Pearce was asked to preach at the opening of a Baptist meeting-house in Guilsborough, Northamptonshire. The previous meeting-house had been burnt down at Christmas 1792 by a mob hostile to Baptists. Pearce had spoken in the morning on Psalm 76:10 ('Surely the wrath of man shall praise thee: the remainder of wrath shalt thou restrain'). Later, during the midday meal, it was quite evident from the conversation that Pearce's sermon had been warmly appreciated. It was thus no surprise when Pearce was asked if he would be willing to preach again the following morning. 'If you will find a congregation', Pearce responded, 'I will find a sermon'. It was agreed to have the sermon at 5.00am so that a number of farm labourers who wanted to hear Pearce preach could attend before their day's work commenced.

After Pearce had preached the second time, and that to a congregation of more than 200, he was sitting at breakfast with a few others, including Andrew Fuller. The latter remarked how pleased he had been with the content of his friend's sermon, but that the sermon seemed poorly structured. 'I thought', said Fuller, 'you did not seem to close when you had really finished. I wondered that, contrary to what is usual with you, you seemed, as it were, to begin again at the end — how was it?' Pearce's response was terse; 'It was so; but I had my reason'. 'Well then, come, let us have it', Fuller responded jovially. Pearce was reluctant to divulge the reason, but after a further entreaty from Fuller, consented.

Love for sinners

He related the following, which was put into print many years later by one who was present on the occasion.

'Well, my brother, you shall have the secret, if it must be so. Just at the moment I was about to resume my seat, thinking I had finished, the door opened, and I saw a poor man enter, of the working class; and from the sweat on his brow, and the symptoms of his fatigue, I conjectured that he had walked some miles to this early service, but that he had been unable to reach the place till the close. A momentary thought glanced through my mind — here may be a man who never heard the gospel, or it may be he is one that regards it as a feast of fat things; in either case, the effort on his part demands one on mine. So with the hope of doing him good, I resolved at once to forget all else, and, in despite of criticism, and the apprehension of being thought tedious, to give him a quarter of an hour.'

As Fuller and the others present at the breakfast table listened to this simple explanation, they were deeply moved by Pearce's evident love for souls. Not afraid to appear as one lacking homiletic skill, especially in the eyes of his fellow pastors, Pearce's zeal for the spiritual health of *all* his hearers had led him to minister as best he could to this 'poor man' who had arrived late.

9. MY DEAR SARAH

In Jane Austen's novel *Northanger Abbey*, one of the characters, Catherine Morland, states that history 'tells me nothing that does not either vex or weary me. The quarrels of popes and kings, with wars or pestilences, in every page; the men all so good for nothing, and hardly any women at all!' Examination of the history books of Austen's era would soon confirm the truth of this statement. Only in recent days has there been sustained interest in the lives of Christian women. Earlier generations may have been slow to recognise the important — and biblically legitimate — roles women have played in the life of the church. But we cannot avoid the fact that God has given women rich ministries down through the history of the church, ministries that are fully consistent with the biblical pattern of male eldership. Among these responsibilities is that of keeping house and raising children to God's glory. It was such a ministry that God gave to Sarah Pearce (d. 1804).

Sarah Pearce

Sarah Hopkins was a third-generation Baptist. Her father was Joshua Hopkins (d. 1798), a grocer and a deacon in Alcester Baptist Church, Warwickshire, for close to thirty years. Her maternal grandfather was John Ash (1724-1779), the noteworthy pastor of the Baptist cause in Pershore, Worcestershire. Sarah met Samuel Pearce (see Chapter 8) soon after he arrived in Birmingham, and they were soon deeply in love. As he wrote to her on 24 December 1790, 'Were I averse to writing ... one of your dear Epistles could not fail of conquering the antipathy and transforming it into desire. The moment I peruse a line from my Sarah, I am inspired at the propensity which never leaves me, till I have thrown open my whole heart, and returned a copy of it to the dear being who long since compelled it to a *voluntary surrender*, and whose claims have never since been disputed'.

They were married on 2 February 1791. Pearce's understanding of what should lie at the heart of their marriage finds expression in a letter written to his future wife shortly before their wedding: 'may my dear Sarah and myself be made the means of leading each other on in the way to the heavenly kingdom and at last there meet to know what even temporary separation means no more'.

Esteem

Pearce's love for his wife deepened with the passing of the years. Three and a half years after their marriage, he wrote to her from Plymouth; 'O, my Sarah, had I as much proof of my love to Christ as I have of my love to you, I should prize it above rubies'. And when Pearce was away on a preaching trip in London in 1795 he wrote to tell her that 'every day improves not only my tenderness but my *esteem* for you'. On the same trip he called her 'the dearest of women — my invaluable Sarah'. In another letter written about the same time he informed the 'partner of my heart' that his letter was a 'forerunner of her impatient husband who weary with so long an absence [longs] again to embrace his dearest friend'. The following year, on an extensive preaching trip in Ireland, he wrote from Dublin on 24 June 1796:

'Last evening ... were my eyes delighted at the sight of

a letter from my dear Sarah ... I rejoice that you, as well as myself, find that "absence diminishes not affection". For my part I compare our present correspondence to a kind of courtship, rendered sweeter than what usually bears that name by a *certainty of success*. And then towards the end of the letter he added, 'O our dear fireside! When shall we sit down toe to toe, and tête à tête again — Not a long time I hope will elapse 'ere I re-enjoy that felicity'.

Passion for God

That Sarah felt the same towards Samuel is seen in a letter she wrote after her husband's death to her sister Rebecca. Rebecca had just been married to a Mr Harris and Sarah prayed that she might 'enjoy the most uninterrupted happiness ... (for indeed I can scarce form an idia [*sic*] ... this side of Heaven of greater) equal to what I *have* enjoyed'.

One final word about Samuel and Sarah's marriage needs to be said. What especially delighted Pearce about his wife was her passion for God. As he told her in the summer of 1793, in response to a letter he had received from her, 'I cannot convey to you an idea of the holy rapture I felt at the account you gave me of your soul prosperity'.

Support for the BMS

Let us return for a moment to Samuel Pearce himself. Given his ardour for the advance of the gospel, it is only to be expected that Pearce would be vitally involved in the formation, in October 1792, of what would become the Baptist Missionary Society (BMS), the womb of the modern missionary movement. In fact, by 1794 Pearce was so deeply gripped by the cause of missions that he was convinced that he should offer his services to the society and go to India. There he planned to join the first missionary team the society had sent out, namely, William Carey and John Thomas. But it was not to be. The executive of the BMS, mostly composed of Pearce's friends, felt that Pearce occupied a post too important to leave for India. And so Pearce and his wife stayed in Birmingham. Pearce spent much of the remaining years of his life raising support, both prayer and financial, for the missionaries in India.

One of the meetings at which Pearce preached saw William Ward (1769-1823) — later to be one of the most valuable of Carey's co-workers in India — accepted as a missionary with the BMS. Those attending the meeting (at Kettering on 16 October 1798) were deeply stirred by Pearce's passion and concern for the advance of the gospel. He preached 'like an Apostle', Andrew Fuller later wrote to Carey. And when Ward wrote to Carey, he told his future colleague that Pearce 'set the whole meeting in a flame. Had missionaries been needed, we might have had a cargo immediately'.

Neglecting to rest

Returning to Birmingham from this meeting Pearce was caught in a heavy downpour of rain, drenched to the skin, and subsequently developed a severe chill. Neglecting to rest, and thinking that what he called 'pulpit sweats' would effect a cure, he continued a rigorous schedule of preaching, both at Cannon Street and in outlying villages around Birmingham. His lungs became so inflamed that Pearce had to ask Ward to supply the Cannon Street pulpit for several months during the winter of 1798-1799.

By the spring of 1799 Pearce was desperately ill with pulmonary tuberculosis. Leaving his wife and five children, he went to the south of England from April to July in the hope that rest there might effect a cure. But absence from his family only aggravated his suffering. Writing from Plymouth to Sarah — 'the dear object of my tenderest, my warmest love' — he requested her to 'write me as soon as you receive this' and signed it 'ever, ever, ever, wholly yours'. Three weeks later he sent Sarah 'a thousand and ten thousand thousand embraces', and added poignantly: 'may the Lord hear our daily prayers for each other!'

Sarah and the children had gone to stay with her family in Alcester, twenty miles or so from Birmingham. But by mid-May Sarah could no longer bear being absent from her beloved. Leaving their children with friends, she headed south in mid-May, where she stayed with her husband until the couple slowly made their way home to Birmingham in mid-July. By this time Samuel's voice was so far gone that he could not even whisper without pain in his lungs.

Closer to Christ

His suffering, though, seemed to act like a refiner's fire to draw him closer to Christ. 'Blessed be his dear name', he said, not long before his death, 'who shed his blood for me ... Now I see the value of the religion of the cross. It is a religion for a dying sinner ... Yes, I taste its sweetness, and enjoy its fulness, with all the gloom of a dying-bed before me; and far rather would I be the poor emaciated and emaciating creature that I am, than be an emperor with

every earthly good about him, but without a God'. Some
of his final words were for Sarah; 'I trust our separation
will not be forever … we shall meet again'. He fell asleep
in Christ on Thursday 10 October 1799. William Ward,
who had been profoundly influenced by Pearce's zeal and
spirituality, well summed up his character when he wrote
not long before the latter's death:

'Oh, how does personal religion shine in Pearce! What
a soul! What ardour for the glory of God! … you see in him
a mind wholly given up to God; a sacred lustre shines in his
conversation: always tranquil, always cheerful … I have seen
more of God in him than in any other person I ever met'.
At the heart of Pearce's spirituality, both lived and taught,
was the theological conviction that 'real religion consists
in supreme love to God and disinterested [i.e. impartial]
love to man'. Measured by this standard, there seems little
doubt about the reality of Pearce's Christian faith and
spirituality. There is also little question of the challenge it
poses to Christians today.

As gold refined

Sarah survived him less than five years. It was a very difficult
time for her, for she buried two of their five children in that
time and keenly missed her husband, who had been her best
earthly friend. Some extracts from her letters follow that
reveal the sterling nature of her Christianity. Her faith has a
very human face as she wrestles with grief and widowhood,
but it is also one that is imbued with the joy of knowing
Christ and the hope of spending eternity with him. Sarah
went to be with her Lord and Samuel on 25 May 1804.

To Mrs H.
25 December 1799

This letter was written but eleven weeks after her husband's death. Sarah was left with five children but her eldest son William was at this time away from home, having gone to live with a Pastor William Nichols of Collingham, near Nottingham. William eventually went to India as a missionary.

'In vain, alas, in vain I seek him whose presence gave a zest to every enjoyment! I wander about the house as one bereft of her better half. I go into the study — I say to myself, "There is the chair he occupied, there are the books he read; but where, oh where is the *owner*?" I come into the parlour — there my tenderest feelings are awakened by four fatherless children. The loss of him with whom I have been accustomed to go up to the house of God diminishes, ah, I may say too frequently *deprives* me of, my enjoyment while there'.

To Mrs F.
11 July 1800

This was written from her home town of Alcester, not far from Birmingham, when her youngest child, Samuel, died.

'After an illness of a few days, it hath pleased the great Arbiter of life and death to bereave me of my dear little boy, aged one year and six months, and thus again to convince me of the uncertainty of all earthly joys and bring to remembrance my past sorrows. He was in my fond eyes one of the fairest flowers human nature ever exhibited; but ah, he is dropt at an early period! Yet the hope of his being transplanted into a more salutary clime, there to re-bloom in everlasting vigour, and the reflection that if he had lived, he had unavoidably been exposed to innumerable temptations, from which if my life was spared, I should yet be unable to screen him, make me still. Though I feel as a parent and I hope as a Christian, yet I can resign him. Oh could I feel but half the resignation respecting the loss of my beloved Pearce! But I cannot. Still bleeds the deep, deep wound; and a return to Birmingham is a return to the most poignant feelings. I *wish* however to resign him to the hand that gave and that had an unquestionable right to take away. Be still then every tumultuous passion, and know that he who hath inflicted these repeated strokes is God: that God whom I desire to reverence under every painful dispensation, being persuaded that what I know not now, I shall know hereafter'.

To Mrs H.
19 September 1801

'It is an unspeakable mercy that I am in the hands of so kind and good a God, who knoweth our frame and remembereth that we are but dust. As a father pitieth his children, so the Lord pitieth them that fear him. How light and trifling do all our trials appear when compared with the important end they are designed to answer. What are the sufferings of the present time compared with the glory that is to be revealed in us? May we be made willing to do and suffer the whole of God's will, in order to our meetness for the inheritance of the saints in light! O that my heart were more in heaven, where I trust my treasure is! At times I can say,

"Do with me, Lord, as seemeth thee good; only sanctify thy dealings with me, and bring me forth as gold refined from all remaining dross".

Most of the letters cited are from one of the following three sources, all of which are housed in the Angus Library, Regent's Park College, University of Oxford: Samuel Pearce Mss; the Samuel Pearce Carey Collection — Pearce Family Letters; the Pearce-Carey Correspondence 1790-1828. For permission to use these letters I am indebted to Regent's Park College, University of Oxford.

10. JOHN SUTCLIFF
AND
THE PRAYER CALL OF 1784

Among the Calvinistic Baptists of the late eighteenth century, one of the most important figures is also one of the least known — John Sutcliff (1752-1814), pastor of the Baptist church in Olney, Buckinghamshire, for thirty-nine years. Sutcliff was an extremely close friend of Andrew Fuller and William Carey and was one of the founders of the Baptist Missionary Society. He played a central part in bringing revival to the English Calvinistic Baptists, far too many of whose churches were somewhat moribund in the mid to late eighteenth century.

Formative influences

He was born on 9 August 1752, to Daniel Sutcliff and his wife Hannah, on a farm called Strait Hey, two miles east of Todmorden, West Yorkshire. The Sutcliffs, both ardent Baptists, attended nearby Rodhill End Baptist Church, which had been planted by William Mitchel (see Chapter 2). But since there was a service at Rodhill End only alternate weeks, the Sutcliffs also worshipped at Wainsgate Baptist Church, near Hebden Bridge. Sutcliff's parents 'were remarkable for their strict attention to the instruction and government of their children', and Sutcliff became acquainted with the truths of Christianity from an early age. Sutcliff was converted as a teenager in 1769 through the ministry of John Fawcett (1740-1817), then pastor at Wainsgate. Fawcett himself was a child of the Evangelical Revival, having been converted under the preaching of George Whitefield and shaped as a young Christian by the Anglican Evangelical William Grimshaw (1708-1763).

Baptised by Fawcett soon after his conversion, Sutcliff joined Wainsgate Baptist Church on 28 May 1769. For the next couple of years Fawcett acted as Sutcliff's mentor, giving him both academic and spiritual instruction. Sutcliff thus received his earliest nurture in the Christian faith from one who was very appreciative of the Evangelical Revival.

Bristol Baptist Academy

Sutcliff's evident hunger for theological knowledge, coupled with a desire to put that knowledge into practice, prompted Fawcett and the Wainsgate Church to encourage him to pursue formal study at the Bristol Baptist Academy. He studied there from 1772 to 1774. The principal teachers at the Academy at that time were Hugh Evans (1713-1781) and his son Caleb Evans, both of whom had a reputation for being evangelical Calvinists.

Caleb Evans was also a fervent admirer of the writings of the New England theologian Jonathan Edwards. He strongly recommended Edwards' writings to his students, describing him as 'the most rational, scriptural divine, and the liveliest Christian, the world was ever blessed with'. Evans was not the only Calvinistic Baptist of his day to be deeply impressed by Edwards. John Fawcett had read Edwards' works in the 1760s and appears to have encouraged Sutcliff to do the same. It is no surprise, then, that after the Scriptures, Edwards' writings exercised the greatest influence in shaping Sutcliff's theological perspective.

Committed to Calvinism

So great was the impact of Edwards on Sutcliff, that after the latter's death there were some who said, 'if Sutcliff … had preached more of Christ, and less of Jonathan Edwards, [he] would have been more useful'. In defence of his departed friend, Andrew Fuller replied, 'If those who talk thus, preached Christ half as much as Jonathan Edwards did, and were half as useful as he was, their usefulness would be double what it is'. More than any other eighteenth-century author, Edwards showed Sutcliff — and fellow Baptists like Fawcett, Evans and Fuller — how to combine a commitment to Calvinism with a passion for revival, fervent evangelism, and experimental religion.

Sutcliff set out from Wainsgate for Bristol in the depth of winter 1772. To save money for the purchase of textbooks, he walked the entire distance, a journey of some 200 miles. Afterwards, it seems, he often travelled on foot, primarily with a view to saving money for books. Indeed, in his latter years, he had accumulated a considerable library, of which the greater part consisted of choice theological works. Andrew Fuller once described it as 'one of the best libraries in this part of the country'. During his two and a half years under the tutelage of Hugh and Caleb Evans, Sutcliff had an outstanding academic record. He also had occasion to preach in various churches in the neighbourhood of Bristol, one of which, at Trowbridge, sought unsuccessfully to call him as their pastor.

Olney

Upon leaving Bristol in May 1774, Sutcliff spent six months ministering at the Baptist church in Shrewsbury, and then another six at Cannon Street Baptist Church in Birmingham, where Samuel Pearce (see Chapter 8) would be the pastor. In 1775 he came to the small town of Olney in Buckinghamshire for a ministry that would last until his death in 1814. Sutcliff was ordained on 7 August 1776. Among the Baptist pastors who took part on this occasion were John Fawcett, who received Sutcliff's confession of faith, and Caleb Evans, who delivered a charge to Sutcliff based on Hebrews 13:17. It was also during 1776, at the annual meeting of the Northamptonshire Association, that Sutcliff first met Andrew Fuller and soon discovered him to be a kindred spirit.

The initial years of his ministry, however, were trying ones. Sutcliff's evangelical, Edwardsean Calvinism deeply disturbed some of his congregation. They saw it as a departure from 'orthodoxy' — they appear to have had Hyper-Calvinistic tendencies — and began to absent themselves from the Lord's Supper and from church meetings. But Sutcliff was not to be deterred from preaching biblical truth. Matters came to a head towards the end of 1780.

Prudent perseverance

At a Church Meeting on 7 December the dissidents declared that the reason for their conduct was their 'dissatisfaction with the Ministry'. After a long debate, it was agreed to let the matter rest for four months, and if the dissidents took their places at the Lord's Table the matter was to be forgotten. Although it took more than four months, Sutcliff, 'by patience, calmness, and prudent perseverance', eventually won over all the dissidents. Fuller would later point to the patience and prudence Sutcliff exhibited on this occasion as a prominent feature in his character. Fuller said, 'Whatever might have been his natural temper, it is certain that *mildness* and *patience* and *gentleness* were prominent features in his character ... It was observed by one of his brethren in the ministry ... that the promise of Christ, [namely] that they who learned of him who was "meek and lowly in heart should find rest unto their souls" [Matthew 11:29] was more extensively fulfilled in Mr Sutcliff than in most Christians'.

In the 1780s Sutcliff became increasingly involved in the affairs of the Northamptonshire Association of Baptist Churches, to which his church belonged. He drew up the circular letter that the association sent annually to its member churches, both in 1779 (on the subject of divine providence) and 1786 (on the Lord's Day). And in 1784 he presented to the association a proposal that would have far-reaching implications.

Edwards' *Humble Attempt*

Earlier that year Sutcliff had acquired a treatise by the North American theologian Jonathan Edwards entitled *An Humble Attempt to Promote Explicit Agreement and Visible Union of God's People in Extraordinary Prayer, For the Revival of Religion and the Advancement of Christ's Kingdom on Earth*. In this treatise, first published in 1748, Edwards appealed for the establishment of regular prayer meetings where there could be fervent prayer that God 'would appear for the help of his church, and in mercy to mankind, and pour out his Spirit, revive his work, and advance his spiritual kingdom in the world'.

The treatise came to Sutcliff through John Erskine (1721-1803), who had corresponded with Edwards in his younger years and was the minister of the historic church of Old Greyfriars, Edinburgh. Erskine has been well described as 'the paradigm of Scottish evangelical missionary interest through the last half of the eighteenth century'. From 1780 till his death in 1803 Erskine regularly corresponded with Sutcliff's close friend John Ryland Jr. — he also wrote occasionally to Sutcliff — sending Ryland not only letters but also on occasion bundles of interesting publications which he happened to receive. So it was that in April 1784 Erskine dispatched to Ryland a copy of Edwards' *Humble Attempt*. Ryland in turn shared it with his friends Sutcliff and Andrew Fuller.

The prayer-call of 1784

Sutcliff was so impressed by this treatise that at the next meeting of the Baptist churches of the Northamptonshire Association he proposed that monthly prayer meetings be established to pray for the outpouring of God's Spirit and the revival of religion. This proposal was adopted by the representatives of the twenty or so churches of the association. It was attached to the circular letter sent out that year and called for them 'to wrestle with God for the effusion of his Holy Spirit'. Practical suggestions on how to implement these monthly meetings followed. It was recommended that there be corporate prayer for one hour on the first Monday evening of each month. The call then continued:

'The grand object in prayer is to be, that the Holy Spirit may be poured down on our ministers and churches, that sinners may be converted, the saints edified, the interest of religion revived, and the name of God glorified. At the same time remember, we trust you will not confine your requests to your own societies [i.e. churches] or to your own immediate connection [i.e. denomination]; let the whole interest of the Redeemer be affectionately remembered, and the spread of the gospel to the most distant parts of the habitable globe be the object of your most fervent requests. We shall rejoice if any other Christian societies of our own or other denominations will unite with us, and do now invite them most cordially to join heart and hand in the attempt'.

Noteworthy points

There are at least three noteworthy points about this call to prayer, which Sutcliff had undoubtedly helped to write. First, there is the conviction that reversing the downward trend of the Calvinistic Baptists could not be accomplished by mere human zeal, but must be effected by an outpouring of the Spirit of God. As Sutcliff later observed in another writing:

'The outpouring of the divine Spirit ... is the grand promise of the New Testament ... His influences are the soul, the great animating soul of all religion. These withheld, divine ordinances are empty cisterns, and spiritual graces are withering flowers. These suspended, the greatest human abilities labour in vain, and the noblest efforts fail of success'. In both this text and that of the circular letter cited above, there is evidence of a theology of radical dependence on the Spirit, a recognition that the Spirit is the true agent of renewal and revival.

Second, there is the inclusive nature of the recommended praying. As the Calvinistic Baptists of the Northamptonshire Association gathered to pray together they were urged to direct their thoughts beyond the confines of their own churches and denomination, and embrace in prayer other Baptist churches and other denominations. In fact, churches of other denominations, along with those of other Baptist associations, were encouraged to join them in praying for revival.

Third, there is the distinct evangelistic or missionary emphasis. The readers of this prayer-call are encouraged to pray that the gospel be spread 'to the most distant parts of the habitable globe'.

Jealousy for the Lord of hosts

Another text that draws together these themes of prayer and evangelism is found in what appears to be Sutcliff's only extant sermon, *Jealousy for the Lord of Hosts illustrated*. It was preached on 27 April 1791 to a gathering of the ministers of the Northamptonshire Association at Clipston, Northamptonshire. The sermon was based on 1 Kings 19:10 — in particular Elijah's statement: 'I have been very jealous for the Lord God of hosts'. Sutcliff first explores the historical context surrounding the statement. He comes to the conclusion that while Elijah's statement contains a 'degree of impatience ... and murmuring', his jealousy for God is commendable, because such jealousy 'enters deep into, and is integrated in the very soul of true Christianity'. Sutcliff proceeds to detail the ways in which such a jealousy manifests itself. As he does so, two characteristics come to the fore.

First, Sutcliff lays great stress on the vital importance of bringing the entirety of one's beliefs and life into conformity with the revealed will of God as found in the Scriptures. True jealousy for God is accompanied by a reverent obedience to God's Word.

Second, he emphasises the visible extension of 'the empire of Jesus'. True jealousy for God is revealed in a love for men which 'can embrace a globe' and which longs that 'the earth be filled with the knowledge of the glory of the Lord'. Such a longing is first expressed in 'fervent prayer for the outpouring of the divine Spirit ... Anxious to see the advancement of the Redeemer's kingdom, you will give vent to your fervent desires by warm addresses at a throne of Grace'.

Third, this jealousy is seen in an evangelistic lifestyle that takes seriously God's desire for his people to be the salt and light of the world. Reflecting on the calling of all God's people Sutcliff declares, 'Are they not the *salt* of the earth? It is not proper that the *salt* should lie all in one heap. It should be scattered abroad. Are they not the *light* of the world? These taken collectively should, like the Sun, endeavour to enlighten the whole earth. As all the rays, however, that each can emit, are limited in their extent, let them be dispersed, that thus the whole globe may be illuminated. Are they not *witnesses* for God? It is necessary they be distributed upon every hill, and every mountain, in order that their sound may go into all the earth, and their words unto the ends of the world'.

Balance

In commending this balance of ardent prayer and vigorous evangelistic effort, Sutcliff was not only describing what he regarded as characteristics of genuine Christianity but he was also outlining measures he considered essential for revival. When these marks of true jealousy for God are present, he concludes, 'This will tend to promote the interests of religion in the world. The cause of Christ will prosper; he must increase; his kingdom shall come. But, though he is indebted to none, he kindly condescends to employ his people in accomplishing these glorious purposes... Under the divine smile, Satan will fall before you like lightning from heaven; his power be broken; his policy confounded: while the empire of Jesus shall advance; his kingdom arise; and the crown flourish upon his head'.

The sermon's significance

One cannot help but notice 'the mood of expansion and optimism' which pervades this conclusion to Sutcliff's sermon, a mood that is present throughout much of the discourse. Little wonder, then, that this sermon was later recognised as a key step on the road to the formation of the Baptist Missionary Society in 1792. This same mood also permeates the prayer call of 1784, as F. A. Cox (1783-1853) was quick to discern when writing on the 50th anniversary of the founding of the BMS:

'The primary cause of the missionary excitement in [William] Carey's mind, and its diffusion among the Northamptonshire ministers [was] ... the meeting of the association in 1784 ... [when] it was resolved to set apart an hour on the first Monday evening of every month, "for extraordinary prayer for the revival of religion, and for the extending of Christ's kingdom in the world". This suggestion proceeded from the venerable Sutcliff. Its simplicity and appropriateness have since recommended it to universal adoption; and copious showers of blessings from on high have been poured forth upon the Churches.'

Revival

Three years after this sermon at Clipston, Northamptonshire, the London Baptist minister John Rippon (1751-1836) printed a list of Calvinistic Baptist congregations and ministers in his *Baptist Annual Register*. Rippon calculated that there were at that time 326 churches in England and 56 in Wales — more than double the number forty years previously. In 1798 he issued another list, according to which there were now 361 churches in England and 84 in Wales. Commenting on these statistics, Rippon stated, 'It is said, that more of our meeting houses have been enlarged within the last five years, and more built within the last fifteen, than had been built and enlarged for thirty years before'. This is no exaggeration. While there was steady growth throughout the last forty or so years of the eighteenth century, the most rapid expansion of the denomination took place in the final decade of the century.

This rapid influx of new converts, which continued unabated into the early decades of the nineteenth century, raised concerns regarding their integration into existing congregations or their establishment in new ones. The presence of these concerns can be seen, for example, in the fact that most of the circular letters issued by the Northamptonshire Association during the last fifteen years of Sutcliff's life dealt with church issues. Moreover, all four of the circular letters which Sutcliff wrote for the association in this period are focused, to one degree or another, on such issues. *Qualifications for Church Fellowship*, written in the year 1800, is a good representative in this regard.

Not just theory

It is evident from the beginning of the tract that Sutcliff is not dealing with a merely theoretical issue. The churches in his association are receiving new members. 'A pleasing business', he remarks, but one that requires caution, 'lest you be crowded with characters who, instead of being a blessing among you, will be the bane of your societies ... [and also requires] tenderness, lest contrary to our Lord's example you break the bruised reed, or discourage the weaker part of his sincere disciples'.

His readers especially needed caution because, in Sutcliff's opinion, 'many, once large and flourishing churches' are now in ruins because of 'a want of due attention to the character of such as they admitted into their communion'. The Holy Spirit, he said, was grieved and withdrew 'his divine influences from [their] sacred ordinances'. Sutcliff does not specify the particular churches he had in mind here. Most likely they were those Nonconformist congregations that, during the course of the eighteenth century, had succumbed to either Arianism (the denial of Christ's full deity) or Unitarianism (the denial of the Trinity).

Church membership

Who, then, should be received into the membership of a local church? Although Sutcliff tackles this question from both the viewpoint of the prospective member and that of the congregation, the essence of his response in both cases is the classical Nonconformist answer — visible saints. 'A Christian society', he declares, 'is styled *a spiritual house; a holy priesthood; a holy temple; a habitation for God, through the Spirit* ... Those who are proper characters to be received into communion with a Christian church, should be spiritual men ... men disposed to seek the good of the interest of Christ in general, and of that society to which they unite in particular; men devoted to God; men who hold fast the form of sound words; and who in their spirit and walk, adorn the doctrine of God our Saviour'.

Sutcliff proceeds to defend at length the practice of requiring prospective members to give an account of their personal religious experience. Mere acknowledgement of the truth of leading Christian doctrines is not sufficient; a profession of 'personal experimental religion' is required. He refers to Jonathan Edwards' controversial *An Humble Inquiry into the Rules of the Word of God, concerning the Qualifications requisite to a Complete Standing and Full Communion in the Visible Church of God*. He comments, 'That great writer has ably proved that nothing deserves the name of a Christian profession where the thing professed is not genuine personal Christianity'. Along with such a profession, Sutcliff insists, there must be a demonstrable 'obedience to all the commandments of Jesus Christ'.

'I wish I had prayed more'

Fourteen years later, when Sutcliff lay dying in 1814, he remarked to Fuller, 'I wish I had prayed more'. For some time after his friend's death Andrew Fuller ruminated on this statement. He found it rather puzzling, coming as it did from a man who had been at the heart of a prayer movement that had been essential to the revitalisation of the Baptist denomination. But eventually he came up with the following 'exegesis' and application of Sutcliff's words.

"'I wish that I had prayed more". I do not suppose that brother Sutcliffe meant that he wished he had prayed more frequently, but more *spiritually*. I wish I had prayed more for the influences of the Holy Spirit; I might have enjoyed more of the power of vital godliness. I wish I had prayed more for the assistance of the Holy Spirit in studying and preaching my sermons; I might have seen more of the blessing of God attending my ministry. I wish I had prayed more for the out-pouring of the Holy Spirit to attend the labours of our friends in India; I might have witnessed more of the effects of their efforts in the conversion of the heathen'. Whether or not Fuller correctly interpreted Sutcliff's statement, his application certainly resonates with themes dear to Sutcliff's heart — personal renewal, the revival of the church, and Spirit-empowered prayer and witness.